ENEMIES
IN THE
WEST WING

A "DC Seven" Thriller

Carl R. Baker

HALLARD
PRESS

ENEMIES IN THE WEST WING, A "DC Seven" Thriller by Carl R. Baker
Copyright © 2022 Carl R. Baker.

Published by Hallard Press LLC.
www.HallardPress.com   Info@HallardPress.com   352-234-6099
Bulk copies of this book can be ordered at Info@HallardPress.com

A version of *Enemies in the West Wing* was published in 2010 by Barringer Publishing under the title *To Defend Against All Enemies Foreign & Domestic*.

This book is a work of fiction. Names, characters, places, and incidents are products of the author's imagination or are used fictiously. Any resemblence to actual events or locales or persons living or dead is entirely coincidental.

Publisher's Cataloging-in-Publication data

Names: Baker, Carl R., author.
Title: Enemies in the West Wing : a "DC Seven" thriller / Carl R. Baker.
Description: The Villages, FL: Hallard Press, 2022.
Identifiers: LCCN: 2022915944 | ISBN: 978-1-951188-62-7 (paperback) | 978-1-951188-63-4 (ebook)
Subjects: LCSH Presidents--Fiction. | Political corruption--Fiction. | Politics and government--United States--Fiction. | Political fiction. | Thriller fiction. | BISAC FICTION / Political | FICTION / Thrillers / Political
Classification: LCC PS3602.A5852 E64 2022 | DDC 813.6--dc23

Printed in the United States of America.   1 2

ISBN: 978-1-951188-62-7 (Paperback)
ISBN: 978-1-951188-63-4 (EBook)

"Fear the Lord your God and serve him. Hold fast to him and take your oaths in his name."
—Deuteronomy 10:20

United States Constitution: Article II, Section 1:

Before he (the President of the United States) enter on the execution of his office, he shall take the following oath or affirmation:

"I do solemnly swear (or affirm) that I will faithfully execute the Office of the President of the United States, and will to the best of my ability, preserve, protect, and defend the Constitution of the United States."

Federal Law Enforcement Oath of Office:

"I will support and defend the Constitution of the United States against all enemies, foreign and domestic; that I will bear true faith and allegiance to the same; that I take this obligation freely, without any mental reservation or purpose of evasion; and that I will faithfully discharge the duties of the office on about which I am about to enter. So help me God."

Military Commissioned Officer Oath of Office:

"I do solemnly swear (or affirm) that I will support and defend the Constitution of the United States against all enemies, foreign and domestic; that I will bear true faith and allegiance to the same; and that I will obey the orders of the President of the United States and the orders of the officers appointed over me, according to the regulations and the Uniform Code of Military Justice. So help me God."

Other books by Carl R. Baker

BROKEN SUNSHINE
*A Case Study of Elder Abuse
and Exploitation in Florida*

PREFACE

While the reader of this novel may recognize that some of the incidents outlined in the book are true, this book is a work of fiction. The reader should not conclude that President Robert Sanchez or any other character is a real person.

In times of dryness and desolation we must be patient, and wait with resignation the return of consolation, putting our trust in the goodness of God. We must animate ourselves by the thought that God is always with us, that He only allows this trial for our greater good, and that we have not necessarily lost His grace because we have lost the taste and feeling of it.

—Saint Ignatius Loyola (1491–1556)

INTRODUCTION

I would readily admit that this book is a bit unconventional. I did not obey all the rules that other writers seem to strictly follow, so I guess I could be considered a story teller rather than a serious writer. Whether I am good at telling a story is for the reader to decide.

However, I wrote this book with a purpose. Believe it or not, it wasn't political. I spent most of my entire adult life in uniform, both military and law enforcement–two extremely important vocations, where service comes before self. I, like you, love this country for all the opportunities she has given me. This is, and must always remain, the greatest country in the world.

The military does not grant Secret or Top Secret clearances without a full and complete vetting process. Likewise, professional law enforcement agencies will not hire anyone without a comprehensive background investigation of the applicant. The public accepts nothing less. Yet, we allow the President of the United States, the leader of the free world, and many other high government officials, to take the oath of office and give them unlimited access to all our top secrets without any type of affirmation of their character. History has proven time and time again that the ballot box certainly does not give us any reassurance of the loyalty and integrity of our elected officials. Why do we as a country allow this to happen?

Secondly, the terrorist threat against our country today is, quite candidly, overwhelming. Should our national leaders fail to secure our borders, the consequences could be devastating to our nation and our way of life. I only hope it is not too late.

This book is a fact based, fictional story which attempts to give you an idea of the possible consequences of such actions. I wrote this book in a relatively short period of time while recovering from major surgery. With the love and support of family and friends, I actually enjoyed the challenge. If this story gives you an understanding of the consequences of public apathy in selecting our leaders, I have fulfilled my goal.

First, I want to thank the reader for caring enough about our Nation and our Constitution to actually pick up this book and give it a look. Secondly, I want to thank all of those who took the time to review manuscripts and offered their views and edits and made the final product so much better: my wife, Katherine who lovingly helped me so very much in both my recovery and writing; my brothers, Bruce and Paul, and my sister-in-law, Gail, for reviewing the manuscript; Dr. Teri Melton, who spent many hours editing and made some wonderful suggestions; and Jim Wise, who has written so many books, yet took the time to review the manuscript and encouraged me probably more than he realized.

This book is dedicated to the many men and women who serve or have served our country in the military or law enforcement and were sworn to protect us from all enemies–foreign and domestic. And let us not ever forget all those who made the ultimate sacrifice in fulfilling that sworn duty. I personally knew far too many of them.

Greater love has no one than this, that he lay down his life for his friends.
—John 15:13

"Our country is now taking so steady a course as to show by what road it will pass to destruction, to wit: by consolidation of power first, and then corruption, its necessary consequence."
—Thomas Jefferson

CHAPTER 1

Tuesday, August 28

It was 4:00 a.m. There was a chill in the air for late August in Rockville, Maryland. As I ducked under the crime tape in the dimly lit parking lot, I started to feel sick to my stomach, for I knew what I was about to see. I could hear the Rockville Police Captain and the forensic technician talking to me, but I was in my own world and not comprehending what they were saying. Suddenly, the sheet was removed from the upper part of the body. Staring at me was the graying face of a Secret Service Special Agent. Had I not asked him to come to the White House yesterday, certainly he would still be alive. Words cannot begin to express what I was feeling, standing there looking at his lifeless body. He was a good friend.

Our country was in deep trouble, and I knew his murder had to be a game changer; unfortunately, I did not know what direction the country would take.

"When the people fear the government, there is tyranny; when the government fears the people there is liberty."
—Thomas Jefferson

CHAPTER 2

Friday, August 3

WAIT! Who in the hell is that man in the gray suit next to the Secretary of Homeland Security? I know I have seen him before, but that was some time ago. As Special Agent-in-Charge of the White House Detail, I should know everyone on this dais. Someone is going to get their ass chewed for this one. I have never liked surprises. None of the agents around the President seem concerned, so someone in the Secret Service has cleared him and quite obviously, there was a screw up in the normal security procedures.

Before I could ask, my earpiece from my radio came alive. "He's been cleared, Boss, I saw you looking. We were notified at the last minute."

A short applause in the middle of the President's speech brought me back to the reality of the moment. The President was explaining to the nation how he was making our country safer by substantially cutting the defense budget. Personally, I did not see the logic in this; after all, protecting our country and keeping the public safe is the number one objective of the federal government. The borders remain unsecure, and the majority of the American people and many members of Congress were asking that the federal government finally secure our borders. With all his props behind him—the Secretary of Defense, the Secretary of Homeland Security, the Secretary of State, the Chairman of the Joint Chiefs of Staff and more generals and admirals than I could actually count, the President continued with his choreographed speech. Do they believe his every word? They must, or why would they be supporting him? Or are they members of that large silent majority that do not like what is happening, but like me, aren't sure what to do? How many souls are sold in Washington every day?

Robert Sanchez is smart, good looking, Yale-educated and the best public speaker this country has had in decades. And he is a charmer. It is no wonder the country swept him into office with such a landslide victory. His campaign was superbly organized, and wisely using all the technology available in today's world, the campaign broke all records in presidential fund raising and campaign volunteers. And the country was ready for a change. Unfortunately, I do not believe this was the change that the public wanted, but it seems that many have not noticed, and many do not care.

As I returned to my office after the event, I tried to understand why President Sanchez would elect to ignore the security procedures that have been in place for years and were established to specifically protect his life. The Secret Service needs to know all those persons who are in close proximity of the President in order to fulfill their sworn duty. Last minute additions should be rare, not a frequent event. I need to get a better understanding of exactly what the President expects from his White House Detail.

The Secret Service Division was actually created by Congress in 1865 to suppress counterfeit currency. But it was not until after the assassination of President William McKinley in 1901 that Congress directed the Secret Service to protect the President of the United States as one of its key missions. In addition to the physical protection of the President and his family, countless hours are expended by agents on intelligence, advance work on all his travel outside the White House, and threat assessments—all to prevent and identify risks to the President.

Everyone in the Secret Service has one fear so great that it brings chills just thinking about it. While few have ever experienced it, the assassination or attempted assassination of the President of the United States is devastating to the entire country, but even more so to the men and women of the Secret Service. We will do anything and everything to protect our President, including sacrificing our own lives. Ironically, our job can be made much more difficult by the actions of the President. If he follows the procedures and does what we request of him, protection and everyone's safety is generally assured. If he ignores procedures and does not work with us, he risks his own life and the lives of the all the Secret Service agents working to protect him. President Sanchez ignores security procedures, much more so than any other President that I have protected. Why any President would act so callously is beyond my comprehension. It makes no sense.

"Jeff, get in here," I yelled from my office to my Assistant Special Agent-in-Charge Jeffrey Polk as he was walking by. As he sat down, I thought about my next words, because quite frankly, I did not know who to trust. The stranger in the gray suit on the dais had really left me feeling uneasy. In addition, Jeff had been a surprise addition to my staff last month courtesy of the White House Chief of Staff, Stewart Cohn. Evidently, Jeff knew someone in high places. I reviewed his personnel folder in detail and found that 30 days ago he was an Agent in the El Paso Field Office. I saw nothing that justified his promotion ahead of other agents who had more experience and higher performance reports. So far his work has been satisfactory, but I did not like the fact that he and Cohn were so cozy. Perhaps they were grooming him for my position. My only hope was they wait until I retire.

"What's up Boss?" he asked with his usual smile.

"Jeff," I started, "you know me well enough by now to know that I hate surprises. So, who was that gentleman standing next to Secretary Walker?"

"That was James Martino in the flesh, boss, and as of yesterday, he is a member of the White House Staff serving as the Hispanic Liaison Czar. And yes, he is the same James Martino who was on the FBI's Ten Most Wanted List for five years."

"How did he pass the background? Why wasn't I told about his appointment?"

"He got an exemption from the usual security clearance by Cohn and Cohn's assistant sent an email this morning on his appointment. It's probably on your computer," said Polk.

"Thanks Jeff. I knew I recognized him from years ago. I will take care of it from here," I said, trying not to let him see how upset this made me. After he left the room, I could only think, how in the hell can this be taking place in the highest office in the free world? How can we allow criminals and radicals to just roam the halls of the White House? And I didn't like the term "czar." It had no place in our democratic government. It all didn't add up, or maybe to them it did, and I just didn't like their math.

James Martino had operated a major illegal drug operation in Texas for years. During a Drug Enforcement Agency (DEA) raid on one of his homes, gunfire had erupted and two agents had been shot. Martino somehow had escaped. Both agents had lived, but one remained paralyzed and confined to a wheelchair. Six of Martino's cronies were arrested and ten weapons were seized. But the weapon that had been used to shoot the DEA agents was never recovered, and based on the forensic evidence, it is believed that Martino shot the agents. Five years later, Martino was arrested and four weeks after the trial began, a mistrial was declared by the judge based on the actions of two female jurors. Everyone knew that Martino somehow threatened their families, but the prosecutor never could establish enough probable cause for jury tampering and was unable to pursue a case against him. Martino was never retried and several months later, he walked out of jail a free man. Now he sits in an office in the White House, not far from the President.

I immediately called Cohn after Jeff walked out of my office and left a message. As usual, he did not return my call. What exactly was our mission for this President?

"CHARLES R. BURKE, SPECIAL AGENT-IN-CHARGE, UNITED STATES SECRET SERVICE" read the sign on my door. Yet so many Secret Service security procedures were ignored by the President and his senior staff, I did not have the foggiest idea what my duties entailed. I retain full responsibility for the protection of the President, yet I see my authority being eroded by the President's Chief of Staff. I do not understand the reasoning behind this, and I need to have an open, frank discussion with Stewart Cohn so he will understand the risks to the President, and we can have a mutual understanding on protection procedures.

December 1, in two years. That's the day I can retire, and I most definitely will. If I can only make it to then, my financial future will be secured, my two children will be out of college and my wife, Kim, and I will be someplace on the water living the good life.

"A problem well stated is a problem half solved."
—Charles Kettering

CHAPTER 3

SATURDAY, AUGUST 4

The Outer Banks in North Carolina has been our vacation spot for the last twenty plus years. And when possible, we always take the first two weeks of August—sort of the divider between summer and the school year. My 19-year-old daughter Marie will be starting her second year at the College of William and Mary, and Tom, my 21-year-old son is a senior at James Madison University.

And then, there is my wife of 25 years, Kimberly, who has been teaching sixth grade since before we got married. She has told me time and time again how this vacation refreshes her to deal with another ten months of "adolescent education and puberty." We all very much enjoyed our time together and I usually took time to make sure it all went as planned. Keeping the interest of two college students was not always easy, but somehow, we always agreed that the vacations got better every year. Hopefully, this year would be no exception.

Kim and I have had a wonderful life together. After several dates when we were in our early twenties, I was convinced that I had found my lifetime soul mate, and I had. She has been a loving, supportive wife with an independence that no one will deny. In my business, the divorce rate is extremely high, yet our marriage grows stronger with each passing day. I am a very fortunate man and Kim would tell you that she feels the same way. Our children have been a real joy in our life. They are not perfect, but neither Tom nor Marie got in any real trouble or gave us any real problems growing up. They are good students, good athletes and well-liked by their peers. There is no greater joy than watching your children grow and become happy, productive adults and Tom and Marie were certainly heading in that direction.

"Kim, I got everything out of the car," I yelled.

"Good," she replied, "the kids have gone for a walk on the beach and before we do anything else, we are going to sit on the deck and have a glass of iced tea."

"How about a drink?"

"It's not 5:00 yet," Kim said. Years of marriage taught me not to pursue the conversation any further.

"What a beautiful day and what a magnificent view the Lord has provided for us," I began as we were sitting enjoying the late morning sun.

"Are you going to enjoy it?" Kim said and then added, "You have been so uptight about work lately and I just want you to relax, have fun during our vacation and forget about work for two weeks."

"Promise," I said, not knowing if I could really get this whole White House, hell, this whole federal government chaotic mess out of my mind.

The silence was broken with Kim saying "Well?" and by the tone of her voice, I knew the moment I had been dreading for months had finally arrived. And then the bomb dropped. "Are you going to tell me what's going on at work?"

"Kim, you know I can't discuss work and besides, there are so many events taking place, I wouldn't know where to start." My words sounded weak even to me, and I knew this would not end the conversation.

"Why don't we start with President Sanchez," Kim asked. "He seems to be the topic of every news story, every radio talk show and he has appeared on every magazine cover in the world. Does the man ever actually do his job?"

Kim and I had the most open relationship of all the couples we know. In order to keep that relationship, I now had to walk this mine field being careful not to blow us to pieces, but above all, whatever I told Kim, had to be the truth. I hoped to find an exit from this conversation that kept our domestic tranquility but didn't scare the hell out of Kim. Not an easy task.

"Let it suffice to say that this President is like no other President I have ever worked for. He doesn't do anything conventionally and it seems that whatever policies and procedures we have in place are disregarded. That in itself would be enough but adding to that is the fact that it is nearly impossible to get any senior White House staffer to return my call when I have a question or need some information. So that, my dear, leads to enormous frustrations. I just keep thinking of the day when we both will be retired and all this crap will be yesterday's concerns. Until then, I plan to keep my head low and count the days," I said with beads of perspiration dripping from my forehead. Please, please, I thought, let's move on to another subject.

"Are you really going to put work out of your mind and enjoy our vacation?" Kim asked. She appeared concerned, but I hoped her question signaled a close to the subject matter.

"You can count on it!" I said probably too loudly and too quickly. At that moment Kim again proved that she is a wonderful, loving wife and took my hand and led me to our bedroom. We knew the kids would be gone for at least another hour. Perfect, I thought, perfect!

We all had a wonderful afternoon and for the record, the first round of drinks began at 4:00 p.m. As a part of our annual tradition, it was now my job to cook four of the best steaks money could buy, or more realistically, that we could afford, and celebrate another wonderful year of life as a family. As I was standing on the deck with the Atlantic Ocean in full view, lighting the grill, I realized how much I needed this vacation. God, I pray it would not be our last.

There I go again, letting work sneak into our vacation. I can't help it. This President and his cronies are destroying our country as we all sit back and ignore it. Why do I feel so defenseless? Why haven't I stood up and insisted that procedures be followed? That's just not me to sit by and do nothing. I have got to figure out something when I get back to the office. Right now, I am on vacation.

"The steaks are ready!" I shouted, really meaning that I hoped everything else was ready as well. And it was.

This first Saturday night vacation dinner was one of our best feasts yet and the evening hours were spent reminiscing about years past, talking about careers for our two children and what lies ahead. Not surprisingly, our children seemed concerned about the direction of our country—something that they have never before expressed. I knew something had to be done. I only wish I knew what that something was.

SUNDAY, AUGUST 5

Although I used to run on a regular basis, it was never really something I enjoyed. However, I do love early morning walks on the beach. For me it is valuable time alone where I can think clearly, get close to the Lord and seek His guidance. And what a beautiful Sunday morning it was. There was not a single cloud in the sky, a slight ocean breeze, and the water sparkled like millions of diamonds were laid upon its surface. There were very few people walking the beach, probably because of early church services. We always liked to go to the last morning service and then go out for a Sunday brunch. That gave me two hours to walk the beach and that was my full intention. Great country this America! Then why was this bastard trying to ruin it? There I go again. Why can't I get this whole mess out of my mind at least while I am on vacation?

Four miles. That is what I am going to do. I will walk down the beach for two miles and walk the two miles back. That way, I have time for a cup of coffee on the deck with the Sunday paper before getting ready for church.

About a half a mile into my walk, I noticed another man walking much more rapidly than me, in hopes I would presume, of passing me. Not so. I suddenly realized he was trying to catch up to me. "Hey Chuck" were the first words I heard. Next to me on the beach stood James W. Bruce, retired Deputy Director of the FBI and a good friend for many years.

"Jim, what a nice surprise to see you here. How are you?" I responded as I stuck my hand out to shake his.

"I thought that was you, Chuck, and I am assuming this is your annual safari to the beach with the family." He grabbed my hand and shoulder in a sign of fond friendship.

"It is," I replied, "and if you and your lovely bride are here this week, dinner is on me."

"Deal," Jim said, "but I'm buying."

"That isn't necessary, but if that is what it takes to get you to dinner, bend my arm," I joked.

We walked along the beach getting caught up on everything new in our lives. Then came the question. "So, Chuck, how is work?" Jim asked.

I could not help it. I let go. "Jim, you know exactly what it's like. We have ourselves an egomaniac as President who does not believe the Constitution applies to him, follows no laws or rules, because evidently, they do not apply to him either. He appointed czars who have criminal records and who do not have to have a security clearance for reasons that are yet to be explained to me; he has spent money worse than a drunken sailor in port after a year at sea. Plus, he is ending free trade as we know it, and, in my opinion, has an agenda which is bringing this great country of ours down!"

Boy, I felt better now that I got that out, but Jim kept walking, not saying a word.

Finally, after what seemed like hours, but was really only a minute or two, Jim spoke: "You forgot the part where our intelligence community was castrated by initiating that bogus investigation into the actions of the CIA. It was through that fraudulent Attorney General, literally drying up all worldwide sources of intelligence. The White House has also taken most of the enforcement powers away from the federal law enforcement agencies, and made the United States the laughing stock for all terrorists and dictators worldwide."

"Thanks Jim, that made me feel better," I stated sarcastically. I lowered my voice and asked quite seriously, "What in the hell are we going to do?"

"Actually, that is why I came to the Outer Banks," Jim answered, "and Chuck, we are going to need your help."

"What can I do to help and exactly who is 'we'?" were the only words I could get out of my mouth.

Jim then told me his version of how our country is changing. "Chuck, there are a lot of Americans from all walks of life who think like we do and the numbers are growing each day. The problem is that it appears that no one is really doing anything about it. Sure, all the grass root efforts and demonstrations all over the country help, but they are without any mechanism for correction except the ballot box and that is years away, too long a time to prevent the real damage to our country. Step up the demonstrations and we end up with civil disobedience, which I believe would actually please the White House. As this White House has publicly proclaimed—'never waste a good emergency.' The President would surely declare Marshall Law and restrict our free movement throughout the country and certainly our Second

Amendment right to bear arms would be suspended simply on an Executive Order."

"Just like you," I said, "and I think I know you well enough to say this, the thoughts of what is happening to our country keeps me up at night and quite honestly has made me ill. However, Jim, I have an initial question for you. Is the President himself making all these crazy decisions, or is there someone behind the scene giving the President his marching orders? If so, who is that person? Could it be Vice President Whitmore, who has a lot more experience than President Sanchez but often comes from 'left field?' Or could it be Stewart Cohn who has been a part of Washington politics for almost 20 years and is known to favor a socialist agenda? So, who can you really trust these days?"

"Given the President's leadership ability or quite candidly, the lack thereof," Jim said, "I cannot be certain who is calling the shots in the White House."

"Back to the matter at hand," he continued. "I needed to find people with an undeniable love for our country and unquestionable values. The first person who came to mind was Chief Justice John C. Walters. I met with him last week and he feels the same way we do. He suggested I get in touch with Steven Mason, who retired as the US Attorney from the Eastern District of Virginia. He is on board as well. Next I went to General J. Paul Monroe, who as you know, served with the Joint Chiefs of Staff for years and was one of President Reagan's top military and intelligence advisers. Our group has to be small and covert which I will explain in a minute, but I need to fill one more position to complete the loop. We need someone inside the White House and that is why I'm here. Before I get into any more details or allow you to give me your thoughts, let me explain our mission. We have a judge who is a Constitutional expert, a prosecutor, a national intelligence/ military expert, a top law enforcement official who knows his way around Washington and the Congress—that's me if you didn't figure that one out, and hopefully we will have you—our internal spy who just happens to be one hell of a good cop."

I realized what he was asking. That's when I felt it coming over me. I knew my life would never be the same. What about my family? Will they be safe? What about my career? Then again, what about my country? I did not know whether to laugh, cry or throw-up! Will my retirement dreams ever be realized? Then again, if the country keeps heading in the direction it is presently, would I be able to truly enjoy retirement? Can my kids still go away to college next month? What does this all mean?

Jim continued. "What we need to do is gather enough evidence to indict the President and as many of his top advisers as possible and remove them from office as quickly as possible. Sounds simple, but I know it is as difficult as it could possibly be, after all, we're breaking new ground here. And one more caveat— we must do all of this without breaking a single law or violating anyone's Constitutional rights or we will most certainly lose and probably end up in jail or dead and be no better than Sanchez and his cronies. Finally, we do not know to what extremes they will go to maintain their power and complete their mission, whatever that may be. So the stakes are high, there are unknown dangers all around us, we do not know all the players and we have no idea who we can trust outside the five of us. If we succeed we will have saved our nation; if we fail we will be the right wing terrorists who tried to overthrow our government and our families will certainly suffer the consequences. And for these reasons, this will be the most delicate assignment ever conceived in this country. It must be covert to protect our families and all of us need to be more careful than we have ever been. I have classified this assignment as TOP, TOP Secret. So Chuck, what are your thoughts?"

This had all the makings of one of those far out espionage movies or a month's episodes of "24." For whatever reason, all of this did not seem real, but more like a nightmare. I also realized that all my frustrations were directed at the President and actually, even though I worked inside the White House, I really did not know who was calling the shots. The only thought that kept popping in my head was, "Why me?" That wasn't really professional and what does that say about my patriotism. Although this felt like the Twilight Zone, I knew I had to maintain my composure and remember what was at stake here.

My response was almost automatic. "Well Jim, you certainly know how to ruin a guy's vacation. Count me in. I can't go on in this frame of mind and sit back and do nothing. That's not my nature."

After a brief pause, Jim smiled and said, "I knew I could count on you. Let's not even mention any of this until the end of your vacation. Patricia and I are here for just a week. We will get together for dinner one night and for one other afternoon. I would like it if you, Kim and the kids could come over for a cookout. The kids won't be bored. Two of my grandchildren who are in college now will be staying a few days, so I am sure the four of them will have a lot to discuss and adventures to compare. When I get back next week, I will start organizing our first steps. Remember, not a word. We would not want to upset the ladies; they will know soon enough."

As we parted there was only one thought on my mind. What was

I getting myself into? But I knew in my heart, if there was anyone who could pull this off, it was Jim. He had moved up the ranks of the FBI rather rapidly and never forgot where he came from. He was well respected and learned his way around Washington and the Congress. He was known as the "go to" person in federal law enforcement when you needed something, regardless of whether it was a contact or just good advice. And most importantly, he was a good friend.

TUESDAY, AUGUST 14

Every vacation needs at least one rainy day where the entire family is confined to the house and forced to spend the full day together. Today was that day. It makes time for some interesting discussions, but more importantly, it is a good time for talks between father and son and mother and daughter. I was sitting in the recliner reading the paper, when Tom came and sat in the chair beside me. Right then I knew he had something on his mind.

"What's up, son?" I asked to start the conversation.

"Dad, this is my last year of college and I really have no idea what I want to do to earn a living," he told me.

"To begin with," I replied, "this may be your last year as a full time student, but most likely not the end of your college studies. I would expect that someday you will return to school to get your Master's or even your Doctorate. In terms of your work, I would start by thinking of activities you enjoy and attempt to match it with a career."

"How would you feel about me going into the military?" Tom asked.

"As a career or for several years to gain the experience and training?"

"I am not sure; I guess I would sign for two years and see if I liked it. I have also thought about being a cop, but I am leaning toward the state police or a large county or city police department instead of the federal agencies."

"So what's wrong with the Secret Service?" I asked jokingly.

"No offense, Dad, but your job seems awfully boring most of the time and I was looking for something a little more exciting," Tom said with a wry smile.

Without even a slight pause, I said, "I think the best way to make such an important decision is for you to gather all the information you can on all of the branches of the military and then start researching all those police departments that may interest you. Once you have it all together, we can sit down and discuss what organization you believe is best for you. Again, the secret to a successful life is doing your homework, so you have some work to do."

"Thanks, Dad. I'll start on that as soon as I get back to school," Tom said and then turned on the television.

I found Tom's comments and perceptions most interesting. I may be getting paranoid, but I believe he was baiting me to see if I would talk about what was going on in the White House. Never, never underestimate your children!

"Of all the forces that make for a better world, none is so indispensable, none so powerful, as hope. Without hope people are only half alive. With hope they dream and think and work."
—Charles Sawyer

CHAPTER 4

MONDAY, AUGUST 20

Believe it or not, my body enjoyed our vacation. My mind was not always present, but no one really noticed despite my responding to several questions with answers that had absolutely no relevance to what was asked. I am starting to think that has become one of my idiosyncrasies.

Two weeks away and two new czars in the White House. I do not even know how many there are anymore. At this rate, who knows how many czars will be appointed in President Sanchez's term. Well, sir, thank you for helping me get my priorities set for the day. It's time to start my new job.

"Jeff," I said into the phone. "Bring me a complete list of the President's czars and all their backgrounds and security clearances ASAP. I got the expected 'Yes Sir' response, and when the office intercom lit up five minutes later, I was surprised. I thought it would at least take ten minutes.

"Yes, Sue?" I responded to my Office Manager. "Mr. Cohn would like to see you right away," she stated. I am sure he does, I thought. "On my way; thank you," I replied with a confidence I did not feel.

It would take at least five minutes to get to his office which would give me time to finalize my response. I already knew the subject matter. You would think that the Secret Service SAC would have an office closer to the President and his senior staff. After all, I am responsible for keeping them alive. I am one of a host of career agents that would throw my body over his to protect him from that flying bullet. In fact, I know I would despite my personal feelings. I took an oath and that is what guides my conduct. My office used to be much closer than it is now. But President Sanchez has an unusual number of Senior Advisers and someone with more clout wanted my office. End of story. I actually thought the move was to my advantage. Now given my new mission, I think I am at a disadvantage.

"Yes sir, Mister Cohn," I stated officially as soon as I was let into his office. He did not ask me to sit down, so I knew it would be a very brief encounter.

In fact, he never raised his head asking, "Why do you want the czar files?"

I was ready for that one. "Sir I review all the files when anyone fills an office in the White House. It allows me to get to know them through the paperwork and I find that it permits easier interaction when I have to deal with them on an issue."

"And how often do you deal with them?"

"Not on a regular basis, but occasionally," was my response.

He finally looked up at me and closed the conversation by stating, "I am responsible for all the czar files and use them daily. When it slows down around here, I will see to it that you get to review them. Thank you." That was it—end of conversation—end of meeting.

Stewart Cohn was an odd duck. He was a lawyer, which as a group, I generally do not trust. He was not very well organized, except for his dress. He looked like a male model. He was intelligent, articulate in his speech, but always in a rush. He was divorced with no children and lived by himself in a townhouse in Old Town, Alexandria. He always seems nervous around me and I do not understand why. It was no secret to him or anyone else in the White House that I was not pleased with his waiving security checks and background investigations on certain presidential appointees. What I found even more disturbing was the Congress was giving this administration a "free ride" on the failure to follow security procedures by ignoring the issue. There must be hundreds of career federal employees that know this administration is not going about its business by following well established, proven procedures. I am all for streamlining government, but when the safety of our leaders and our country is at stake, I speak up. Why is no one else saying a word? There is this widespread, overwhelming fear of the President and his senior staff that I do not understand. Last I checked, we all put our pants on the same way—one leg at a time.

I took my time walking back to my office and even stopped by the kitchen to get a cup of coffee. I now had two facts that I did not have an hour ago. First, I was never going to see the czar files and second, I could not trust Jeffrey Polk, my Assistant Special Agent-in-Charge. You know, I finally feel like I am again serving my country.

TUESDAY, AUGUST 21

The expected call came early Tuesday morning at exactly 7:28 a.m. Jim knew I always got to the office early; otherwise I would spend half of my day on Interstate 95. It was not a conversation, it was a directive.

"Comfort Inn, Route 3, Fredericksburg, Room 501. 7:00 p.m. tonight."

That was it. This is starting to feel like a James Bond movie and I just received my orders for a new dangerous assignment. Jim wanted covert and covert it would be. I know he is right; I just wish I had all the facts that he obviously possesses. I guess there will be no turning back now.

The next few hours flew by, probably because I was deep in thought of what lay ahead. Do my actions put my family and retirement at risk? Then I thought of the men and women in our military who risk it all each and every day. I had no more doubts; I knew what I had to do.

Knowing Washington traffic as I do, I gave myself two hours for the trip thinking I would be at least 15 minutes early. Wrong. I knocked on the door to Room 501 at exactly 6:58 and when Jim opened the door, I quickly realized that I was the last person to arrive. Duly noted.

Jim made all the appropriate introductions and after several minutes of small talk, we got down to business. The room had been set up in a circle with chairs and use of the bed. Needless to say, last one in, I got the wooden grade school type chair. Jim was the only one with paper and pen, so I immediately put mine under my chair. I should have known that, but hell, at this point I am only a spy-in-training.

Jim started by stating, "Let me remind you why we are all here. We are all very much concerned with the direction our federal government is taking. We do not share the President's vision or value system for America. We do not believe capitalism should be replaced with the redistribution of wealth. We do not believe that the mounting national debt is good for our country. We do not believe the military should be substantially reduced. We do not believe the borders should be unsecure. And we do not like our current foreign policy where we are critical of our friends and apologizing to our enemies.

I would have to say that President Sanchez is a great orator who certainly sounds convincing to the crowds. But his lies know no boundaries and his words are certainly not corralled by the truth. How long can we continue down this road? Why do so many people just accept things as they are? Does the average American see what lies ahead? Certainly many must recognize what is happening to our country. The way I see it, the choices are clear. We can either believe what we see and hear each day and objectively predict the end of America as we know it; we can close our eyes and go on with our own selfish individual lives with the same result; or we can do whatever it takes to save our great nation. So there really is no choice. We have to save America. We are not only five strong. We have to believe that the United States of America is full of true patriots who are in full support of everything we are doing. Together, we can make a difference."

Jim has such a great mind and is so organized or anal, take your choice, that I felt with some confidence that our actions may really make a difference. He continued the gathering just like most organizational meetings—with the ground rules.

Jim came prepared and set up a white board that listed those principles that would guide our actions.

- This group, organization or whatever you think it is does not exist.
- Our individual authority for what we are doing comes from our oath of office "to defend the Constitution of the United States against all enemies, foreign and domestic."
- No one is above the law and that includes all of us.
- There are no politics here. We are seeking the truth—nothing more—nothing less.
- There is no intent here to cause the overthrow or destruction of our government. To do so would certainly be against the Smith Act and certainly result in our arrests. We are only to determine if and what laws are being violated and all information will be presented to a grand jury.
- Meetings in public will be between two people only; three is an exception, but never with four or five.
- Keep as little as possible in writing with the exception of evidence. Remember, dates and times are important.

- All evidence will be hand delivered to me. Use the evidence forms that I will be furnishing. They are generic. Evidence Storage Area TBD (To be determined).
- Start paying for all your personal purchases with cash. Too much information can be gleamed from your use of credit cards—where and when you shop, where and when you eat, what cleaners you use and a host of other personal habits. In other words, all the patterns you have established can be determined from your use of credit cards and from your cell phone.
- Start gradually altering your schedule.
- Calls to private, specified cell phones only. And if you have a cell phone on you right now, take out the battery. We will discuss this later.
- When something applies to this mission it will be DC- related. To everyone else that means the District of Columbia. To us it means "Defending our Constitution."

"For right now, I am trying to keep it simple, but I am sure there will be additions to the list," Jim continued. "About the cell phones, if anyone became suspicious in any way, a quick computer entry would tell the White House where and when we were meeting through the GPS in our cell phones. I have purchased six prepaid cell phones with 500 minutes from six different locations and three different area codes. As I pass them around, take your phone and one of the small cards that has the initials and numbers for each of the others. By the way, both the initials and numbers are reversed. Once you memorize the information on the card, shred it. These phones have been modified to never show the number of the phone or any number you call, or any number that calls you.

"I do not expect that we will have any real large expenses, but you never know. In the meantime, I had some extra money put aside and frankly, I cannot think of a better use for it. I will let you know if it becomes an issue.

"Where do we start? I will give you my thoughts and then open it up. The Judge will be responsible for issuing all the court orders we need— subpoenas, Title III interception orders, and whatever else we need up to and hopefully including arrest warrants. Steve will be our attorney and prosecutor and as such, will be responsible for finalizing any papers we need to file with the court and most importantly, what the charges will be. The General and Chuck will help me in gathering the information and evidence we need to lock these cronies in jail for the rest of their natural lives. Sounds simple, but we are all smart enough to know that it certainly won't be easy.

"One crucial point needs to be stated early in the investigation. I for one, am not certain who is making the decisions in the White House. It would seem to me that the President has the final word, just like past administrations. I do not know that to be the case. Given his inexperience, could it be Vice President Whitmore, or has the President given unlimited decision-making authority to Chief of Staff Stewart Cohn? If we are unable to answer this question, we will not be successful in our mission.

"Who can we trust and who can we absolutely not trust? I am sure there are names popping into your heads as we speak. However, you must be absolute in both categories. If you are not sure, or you have any doubt, do not add that name to either list. Make one mistake, and we are history! As a result, I do not expect a real long good-guy list.

"How do we prepare the public for what we hope is about to take place? Let there be no doubt, the majority of the American citizens are on our side. Talk radio and the cable channels are already helping us here. But in the end, we do not want to create riots in the streets. So be thinking about this."

"And finally," Jim concluded, "I need to share with you that for the first time in months, I am again excited about the great potential of this country and I want to thank each of you for the sacrifices you have made for our great nation, and the ones you are about to make. You are all true patriots!" And with that, Jim sat down.

I looked around the silent room. I saw deep stares and wet eyes. What a moment this was. My only thought went to our founding fathers and how they must have felt when they first decided to write a Declaration of Independence. Suddenly, I knew we were doing the right thing and I knew the Lord would guide us.

General Monroe was the first to break the silence. "I owe this to my country for all she has given me. God Bless America!" And we all responded, "God Bless America!"

General John Paul Monroe was destined to be a soldier. He had decided at age ten that he wanted to go to West Point and that is when his quest began. He worked hard in high school and devoted all his free time to study and sports. He graduated third in his class with four high school letters for sports—football, baseball, basketball and golf. With some help from his Congressman, he received an appointment to West Point in 1961 and graduated number two in his class. He and his high school sweetheart, Cindy, were married the next day and their 40 year military journey began. He was a Captain by the time he saw combat action in Viet Nam. Shortly after beginning his tour, two infantry companies were pinned down by enemy fire and taking heavy causalities. Captain Monroe, who was in the adjacent sector with his infantry company, gathered as many resources as he could, to include air support and responded. Several hours after his arrival, the enemy fled from the intense fire fight and countless soldiers were saved that day. For his actions, the entire Company won a Presidential Unit Citation and Captain Monroe won a Silver Star. That was only one of the events that defined General Monroe's military career which ended with four stars on his collar.

After another hour or so of open frank discussions, we all left the room—one by one. The ride home was euphoric, probably for all of us. After rehashing the entire meeting in my mind, I realized that I truly felt relaxed. Why? Was it because I was accepting the reality of my new assignment? Or was it because there was finally a solution to the major problem this country has been dealing with for months? Either way, it was right to put your country first. How else would we survive as a nation?

WEDNESDAY, AUGUST 22

With so many things going through my mind, the usual 50-minute ride to work seemed like five. The familiar landmarks that I use each morning to gauge my arrival time were missing this morning. I amused myself with the thought that I would have to check this evening on my way home to make sure they are still there. In the meantime, I better spend some time getting my ducks in a row; otherwise, my wandering mind will interfere with my spy duties. Being oblivious to the obvious is both stupid and dangerous.

Rethinking the standards established last night for cell phone usage, I realized they would just not work for me. As far as I can tell, I am the only one in our little group that has to be available 24 hours a day, seven days a week. I made a mental note to talk to Jim about a solution to this problem.

But the larger problem is my assignment to help gather the information and evidence that will eventually lead to the restoration of our Constitutional form of government. What do I already know, what do I need to know and how do I fill the gaps? And making that task even more difficult is that little caveat of doing everything legally and above board. Forget the above board, I was thinking, just keep everything legal. Spies never do everything above board. Shouldn't I have someone overlooking my training here? Hell, I did not even get to attend the Spy Academy!

I hit the intercom button and asked Sue, my secretary, to have Jeff Polk come in. "He's not here today, Mr. Burke," Sue answered. "He called in this morning and told me he was on special assignment, available by cell."

"Oh, that's right. Thanks," I said, covering very quickly. I needn't let my staff know that obviously we had a chain of command problem.

I couldn't dial that number fast enough. "Jeff, exactly where are you right this minute?" I asked in the same tone I would use on someone just arrested.

"I am on a special assignment for Mr. Cohn; he was supposed to call you and give you all the info," Jeff said.

"Well, he didn't, and you never answered my question," I said, a little more civilly.

"I am in the lobby of the Mexican Embassy on Embassy Row, waiting for a meeting on security to start."

"See me when you complete your assignment, no matter how late it is." I ended the conversation with those words.

I rechecked my voice mail—nothing; Blackberry—nothing; email— nothing.

Steve Oates has worked in Technical Support Services his whole career. We were friends and I trusted him. But, should I call him? I would be doing this even if I did not have the "DC" (Defend our Constitution) assignment, I told myself.

"Steve, this is Chuck," I said. "The assignment that I am about to give you reminds me of the mid-1980s when you, Bill Johnson and I were stuck in a hotel room for a month. Does that ring a bell?"

"Boy, do I remember those good old days," Steve said laughingly, "I hope it is exciting; I have been bored out of mind since the change of administration."

"Well, this is the start of something that could prove very interesting." I said, "It is a sealed case with only the two of us authorized any information, understand?"

"You know I do and I like it already."

"At 9:02 a.m. this morning, five minutes ago, I called ASAC Jeffrey Polk's issued cell phone," I said. "I need to know where he was when he received the call and all outgoing calls he made within 15 minutes of that call, to include who he was calling and the location of that individual. That should be pretty easy for you, my friend."

"It's ten minutes of work, Chuck. Criminal or administrative?"

"Administrative for now, Steve, but I will keep you posted.

Thanks!" I said, and hung up the phone.

I sat still for a couple of minutes. In the future, I needed to stop and think out my steps before I react like I just did. This was more than my career on the line. I have a responsibility to at least four other people, and what I just did increased it to five. Steve, whether he knew it or not, just joined a very special group of men. It appears that I never gave him a choice. Again, duly noted.

I glanced at my computer. I had just received an email from Chief of Staff Stewart Cohn stating that he was sorry for the short notice, but he needed to borrow Jeff Polk to fulfill a last minute request from the Mexican Embassy on VIP security. Timely, I thought.

Time to get down to business. What do I know that will help us to complete the most important assignment of our lifetime? There are many unanswered questions surrounding the background of President Sanchez. His association with known felons has been documented time and time again. In fact, the President continues these associations and has even appointed a convicted felon, James Martino, to one of the growing number of White House czars. Obviously, if policies were followed and these czars were vetted, Martino would not have passed the background investigation and most likely, would not receive Senate confirmation. The President has exempted the czar positions from any type of scrutiny, an outright violation, I believe, of the United States Constitution.

The President's association with known terrorists and radicals has likewise been well documented. When the press got too hot on this issue during the campaign, he backed away from these relationships. However, once elected, he appointed a self-proclaimed communist to yet another czar position in White House.

Why would President Sanchez want anyone in the White House that has not been subject to a thorough background investigation? Probably the most important question that needed to be answered is why would the people of the United States of America want anyone to serve as President, the highest position in the free world, without a thorough background investigation?

The sudden ringing of my cell phone broke my train of thought. "Burke," I answered.

"Chuck, Steve here. Ready to copy?" Steve asked.

"Go ahead," I replied.

"Polk was in the Mayflower Hotel on Connecticut Avenue when he took your call. As you know, that's about as precise as I can be on location. He could have been in the lobby or in a room. Two minutes later, he called White House Chief of Staff Stewart Cohn at his townhouse in Old Town. I know you have that address. The call lasted 40 seconds. Five minutes later he called another cell phone belonging to James Martino. You would know better than I, but isn't he one of the President's new czars? That call lasted 18 seconds."

"One and the same," I said, referring to Martino. "Thanks Steve. I am certain that you and I will be having many more conversations."

"Anytime," Steve concluded, "you know I love suspense, intrigue and danger. Talk to you soon."

If you only knew my friend, I thought, if you only knew.

That confirms it. I now have my first three names on my official "Do Not Trust List." On the other hand, based on my past experiences with Steve and knowing how honest he is, I can add him to my trusted list. Three to one—I certainly hope that ratio changes or we are in deep trouble!

With my door now locked, I took my cell phone that Jim had earlier distributed to our group, now affectionately called my "spy phone," and called Jim. After filling him in on the events of this morning, I asked him if there was any possible way we could get copies of any available security video from the Mayflower from 8:00 a.m. to noon this morning. I told him the main entrance and lobby area would be most telling.

I should have guessed. "We can do better than that," Jim said. "The head of security for the Mayflower is a retired FBI agent." Jim was well respected by those who worked with him and most agents, still working or retired, would do most anything he asked.

As expected, Jeff Polk was waiting to see me at exactly 4:00 p.m.. I kept the conversation brief and to the point. I referred him to a specific section in the Secret Service Manual that required him to notify his immediate supervisor anytime that a special assignment would keep him from his assigned duties.

I told him that I was not looking to micro-manage him, I just wanted him to keep me informed when something unusual occurred. He agreed. After some small talk to put him at ease, I asked him how his day went. He told me that it went very well.

I could not help myself. As he was leaving, I stated, "I am glad that everything went well today. I just want you to know, that the next time a Mexican government official gets 'whacked' by a member of one of the drug cartels, I am holding you responsible." I smiled as he walked out the door. I think he was smiling too, or maybe not!

THURSDAY, AUGUST 23

Thursday morning I spent the majority of my time doing those tasks that were outlined for me by the Secret Service in my job description. Damn! I hate that work gets in the way of a part-time spy. It was 11:45 a.m. before I knew it, and I decided to have lunch at my desk and continue to work on my outline on what I knew and what I needed to know. I had just gotten pen to paper when my spy phone began ringing. I answered it with "Hello," remembering that spies never shout their last name into their phones.

"Chuck, James here. How would you like to do some fishing this weekend?" was how Jim Bruce opened the conversation.

"Why do I think this has nothing to do with fishing?" I asked.

"Oh, but it does, and if we are fortunate enough to get our work done, we may have an hour or so to fish, so do bring along your best rod and reel. In any case, we need the props so our wives will not ask any questions," Jim said.

"OK, count me in."

"Here's the deal," Jim continued somewhat enthusiastically. General Monroe has a summer home at Smith Mountain Lake near Roanoke, with a lot of privacy. We all need to get together and figure out a concrete plan. Between the information you have given me on Polk, and others have given me in the last day or two, we have more than enough to get started. And we have our first piece of evidence, compliments of Mayflower security. I am going to rent a nine seat van and everyone can ride with me. We will meet at the Pentagon City Mall south parking lot at 7:00 a.m. on Saturday morning and we will be home about 5:00 p.m. on Sunday.

I will take care of the food. You just bring all the information you have and your thinking cap. We now have a sixth member and he will be joining us as well. And by the way, I think we will have some time to relax and all get to know each other. See you bright and early Saturday morning."

I really did not have any plans for the weekend. The kids left this Tuesday for school, and Kim needed some time to get her act together since she was going back to school for teacher meetings on Monday. A weekend fishing with the guys would be just what the doctor ordered. I had better do some serious work between now and then. I do not want to screw up my probationary period as a spy-in-training and get myself fired.

My lunch was now cold, but it made no difference. I was more interested in getting organized for the weekend, so once more out came my spy notebook which fits conveniently in my inside jacket pocket. Hence, it never leaves my side.

One list I needed was all those who had direct access to the White House, meaning they had a permanent White House ID or a temporary White House ID with an expiration date. If everyone had followed appropriate policy, which I was beginning to question, that list would be on my computer, but restricted to all but a few Senior White House Staffers and the President. The list is 84 pages long, so I downloaded it to my flash drive, which is encrypted. Next, I would need the White House Log which identifies all those who enter the White House and do not have an ID card. Baseball teams, Girl Scout troops, friends and relatives of almost everyone on staff, military personnel, tourists, dinner guests, and politicians come through the doors of the White House every day. This is automated as well; however, it is never up-to-date. For my first attempt at this, it would best to exclude all groups above three. That brought the number down to 8,230 visitors for the first six months of the administration.

Although I was sure there were many, there was one incident on my mind that I needed to get documented. On June 21 at about 9:30 p.m., I was returning to the White House with the President. Normally, once the helicopter lands on the White House lawn, I head for my car and start home, leaving the agents to "tuck the President in." But on this night, I needed to go my office and review the schedule for the weekend due to the sudden illness of one of the agents. I was surprised to see so many lights on in the West Wing, so I went to the Chief of Staff's Office and knocked. When I was asked to come in, they were surprised to see me and I was surprised to see eight men in Cohn's office. I only recognized four of the eight.

"Everything OK, Chief?" I had asked Cohn.

"Thanks, Chuck. We are just working a little later than normal this evening," Cohn replied.

"Have a good night," I said as I closed the door.

Normally, I would not have given this a second thought. I frequently see people in the White House whom I do not recognize. But usually not at this time in the evening unless there is a large social event scheduled. However, I have noticed there have been several other late Thursday evenings in the Chief of Staff's Office and, with my faith and trust in this administration at about zero, I want to look at this further and see if I can find anything unusual. By the way, the President could not have missed all the lights in the West Wing that evening, but he did not seem the least bit concerned.

Unfortunately, I had not checked the White House records that evening or even checked with the Secret Service supervisor present to see if he or she could tell me anything about the meeting. I must have been in an entirely different mindset at that time. Now, quickly checking the June 21 log, the last entry of someone outside of the White House Staff was at 5:20 p.m. and that was an electrician from the General Services Administration and he was escorted the entire time he was inside the White House. Why am I not surprised that there is no official record of their visit?

Looking at my watch, I could not believe it was past six o'clock. Time flies by when you are having fun! Or maybe it flies by when you find yourself doing something you strongly believe in. Or perhaps, I just really like being a spy.

"Poor government comes about when good citizens sit on their hands instead of standing on their feet."
—Robert Baker

CHAPTER 5

SATURDAY, AUGUST 25

I did not sleep all that well last night. Was it the excitement of the day ahead or the feeling that everything appeared to be going smoothly with the spy assignment? Unfortunately, I knew it was both—some excitement and some apprehension. Although Kim thought the fishing trip was a good idea and would help me forget about work for a while, the thought of her alone all weekend troubled me now more than ever. I am not even going there, or I certainly will be crazy by noon.

Given my last trip, I was not going to be the last one today. I wasn't; in fact, I was the first one there. A fresh cup of coffee, a cinnamon roll and this morning's paper, I was good for the 15 minute wait. I had taken my daughter's car this morning leaving the "company" car at home in the garage. Two reasons—my daughter is away at college and the car needs to be driven once a week and there was no way I was going to leave my assigned Secret Service vehicle sitting in a mall parking lot for two days.

Jim arrived first with the van and an African American gentleman sitting in the front passenger seat. Within minutes, all the others arrived and after loading our luggage and, believe it or not, our fishing equipment, we were off. It was obvious Jim was holding off on the introduction of our newest member so he would only have to do it once. As we pulled out of the parking lot, I noticed all our cars were pretty well scattered throughout the lot. Intentional or not, I thought it was a good idea.

Jim started right in. "Gentleman, I would like to introduce you to Joe Wells, retired CIA Intelligence Analyst and probably the finest video/audio technician this country has ever employed. I expect that in order to complete our mission, we are going to need some audio and/or video surveillance; rest assured, the best in the business is now on our team." The whole group applauded and somehow without straining any backs or pulling any muscles, we each shook his hand and introduced ourselves.

Joe told us how pleased he was to be included and how much this country means to him. "I have never been more proud to get an assignment of this magnitude," Joe concluded, "and I promise I will do everything I can legally do to save this country. However, there is something that all of you should know. My wife, Jackie, worked on President Sanchez's campaign and thinks the man walks on water. Obviously, I do not share her views and let it suffice to say that in the name of domestic tranquility, we do not discuss politics in my house. I tell you that because last week the White House told her they may have a position for her working for the Treasury Secretary since her background is in banking. Presently, she is waiting for an offer."

As a spy-in-training, I could not even begin to tell you how thrilled I was to have Joe on board. My job just got much easier. I, for one, was not concerned about Joe's wife working in the Sanchez Administration. I am sure Jim would not have brought him aboard if he had even a slight indication that this would be a problem.

There was a lot of conversation going on in the van, but I was deep in thought and in my own little world. Joe's elevated voice snapped me out of it. "Jim, are we being tailed?" Joe suddenly asked. I could see Joe looking at some unknown piece of technical equipment.

"I have been watching, Joe. I don't think so at this time," reported Jim.

Joe continued, "There are at least eight cell phones in the van right now—seven are on and one is off without the battery being removed."

"Oh shit," I spurted out. "Jim, I have been meaning to talk to you about my need to be available 24/7 and did not know how to handle my Secret Service cell phone."

"Turn it off and remove the battery for now and we will get it straightened out in a minute," Jim ordered.

"Still no tail that I can detect," Jim told Joe.

Steve Mason spoke up, "I forgot to take the battery out of my phone, but I am removing it as we speak."

"Good," Jim replied.

You could hear a pin drop inside the van at that moment. Joe spoke again, "Since we are all together, let's remove the batteries from our generic phones and then we can have a discussion and develop some protocols."

Once that was completed, Jim reported one more time, "No tails unless they are invisible or have air support." I do not know why, but I was relieved, and I was certain all of us felt the same way. However, I knew that 'oh shits' were not good in the spy business.

There were five minutes of relaxed conversation while the General explained the layout of his lake house and told us what rooms each of us would be using. It certainly sounded like a place we could relax and hopefully, get a great deal accomplished. A five bedroom, three and a half bath lake house was certainly beyond my imagination and well beyond my means.

After a minute of silence, Joe returned to the subject of phones. "Chuck," he started, "would it harm anything or interfere with any of your phone use if I disconnected the GPS on your phone? Do you ever use it for Mapquest or as a GPS device when needed?"

"Not really," I said.

"Good, let me have your phone and in five minutes you can turn it back on and not worry about it," Joe told me. He added, "Now the only time your location can be tracked is when you use your phone. Remember that goes for the good guys as well, so if you are ever in trouble and want to be found, keep using the phone. Jim," Joe continued, "that was a good move on your part buying these cheap phones. They are not GPS capable, so the same holds true on tracking locations. However, if one of these phones gets linked to any one of us, it would not be difficult to determine where we are and where and when we meet. I would recommend that for the weekend, we turn the phones on only when we need to use them and that way we protect disclosure of the General's lake house as our meeting place. And for your info, I will also check the house once we get there to ensure our conversations remain private. In fact, I will be checking all your homes and offices next week as well. Now, General, exactly what kind of fish do you have in that lake of yours?"

Before the General could answer, Jim stated, "Now you all know why I included Joe as an extremely valuable member of our group." Cheers and "Amen's" echoed through the van.

Jim was generally taking orders from the General on where to go—not only to get to the lake house, but what roads to use to make sure we had no tails. I couldn't imagine that anybody knew what we were up to for we really hadn't done anything to date. And I was certain no one was concerned about six older gentlemen going fishing. I am being careful here. My best guess was that the General was in his early seventies, the Judge and Jim were in their early sixties and the rest of us were in our mid to late fifties. Steve was probably the youngest of the group. So the term "older gentlemen" seemed appropriate and should offend no one.

I didn't even know we were close to Smith Mountain Lake until Jim pulled down what appeared to be a dead-end street and all at once before our eyes, water sparkled everywhere. I assumed the mountain shooting out of the water in front of us must be Smith Mountain. What a sight! If this is how we were going to spend the next two days, I suddenly felt sorry for the rest of the world.

Judge Walters, who so far appeared to be a man of few words, slapped the General on the back saying, "Paul, looks like you found yourself a piece of paradise here!"

"We have enjoyed it," said the General proudly.

The General insisted we take a tour before we begin to unload the van. While the view was most impressive, the house was not far behind. It was spacious, well decorated and obviously built using only the best in materials and workmanship. It was the type of place you would see in a magazine wishing that you would win the lottery so you could afford it. There was not a room in the house that did not have a view of the lake. I think the entire group was pleasantly surprised.

It only took us 30 minutes to unload the van and get organized. By mid-morning, we were all sitting down with a cup of coffee and a pastry, ready to go to work. The Judge suggested that we spend the first few minutes going over the facts that we believe justify the actions we were about to undertake. I could not think of a better place to start.

"From my point of view," started Judge Walters, "the United States Constitution is the guiding document for government at every level. The founding fathers established three branches of the federal government in order to ensure a balance of power. What is at risk here is that balance. President Sanchez's White House has seized power that constitutionally belongs to the Congress of the United States, by either Executive Order or by his administration's interpretation of a number of laws, most significantly the Federal Reserve Act. In his mind, he has justified the complete control of a number of private institutions, most significantly the banking and automobile manufacturing industries which are private American corporations. Unfortunately, the Judiciary was never included in any of these discussions and has been pushed to the sidelines. The President's quest to further expand and control labor unions throughout the country is wrong and quite honestly, scares the hell out of me. I am here with you today because I am certain that unless we restore the balance of power, our democracy is in its final years."

Chief Justice John C. Walters was a Harvard law graduate who has proven over the years to be a welcomed addition to every court he has served. He is one of those rare individuals with a high degree of intelligence combined with a lot of common sense. He always followed the law, but applied it in a sensible, caring way never ignoring those unique factors of the case. In terms of sentencing, he was extremely fair. However, should you be an unlucky defendant convicted of a third felony in his court, you most likely will have a wall or electric fence surrounding you for the major portion of the rest of your life.

I spoke next. "In addition, President Sanchez has added an unprecedented number of czars that further usurp the balance of power in Washington and gives the President powers far beyond what our forefathers ever imagined. These czars are appointed by the President and are not subject to the scrutiny of a vetting procedure and do not require Senate confirmation according to the President's Chief of Staff. We now have convicted felons and self-proclaimed Marxists walking around the White House. Judge, it seems to me that this practice should be reviewed by the court."

"Let me just say that I believe there is something in the works on this issue," the Judge told us all.

"What concerns me," began General Monroe, "are the President's signs of weakness when dealing with the war on terror, the proliferation of nuclear weapons by Iran and North Korea and the President's worldwide apology tour. We are disappointing our allies, especially Israel, and turning our backs on many of the young democracies that were formerly a part of the Soviet Union. Our status as a world power comes from a strong military and our overt push for democracy throughout the world. President Sanchez is, in my mind, jeopardizing our world standing."

"Let me add that the CIA rank and file feel this President has no appreciation for what they do and has horribly politicized the Agency," said Joe Wells. "By allowing or directing the Attorney General to review the interrogation policies of the CIA, the Agency is at a standstill. Not only because the agents are concerned that their actions could lead to dismissal or even worse, imprisonment, but because foreign governments have ceased sharing intelligence information with the CIA in fear that it will make its way to the New York Times. I cannot begin to tell you how dangerous this is for our country."

Steve Mason jumped right in. "I can tell you that all the federal law enforcement agencies feel they have their hands tied by this administration and they are having much difficulty getting the approval of the Attorney General in hundreds of investigations. Specifically, the US Attorney in El Paso was denied permission to proceed with a major Latino gang investigation and the US Attorney for the Eastern District of Virginia was denied investigative authority for a public corruption case involving a former law partner of Stewart Cohn, the President's Chief of Staff. The number of DEA agents working the Mexican border has been cut in half over the last six months, in spite of the President canceling the Executive Order that permitted the National Guard to assist the Border Patrol on our southern border."

Steve has been a prosecutor his entire career. During law school, he interned with the Commonwealth Attorney's Office in his home county of Fairfax, Virginia. He knew then that he had found his calling. Upon graduation, he was offered an Assistant Commonwealth Attorney position in Fairfax and eventually rose to the number two slot, handling all the major felony cases. He left the Commonwealth Attorney's Office to accept the appointment to the United States Attorney for the Eastern District of Virginia where he served for over eight years. Several months ago, he was replaced by a President Sanchez appointee, as were most of the other United States Attorneys across the country.

The open dialogue continued until after 1:00 p.m. Seeing the need to break for lunch, I added one more point. "With all the animosity and anger that we are seeing throughout the country, the worst case scenario would be if something were to happen to President Sanchez. The consequences would be devastating for the country and the Secret Service is taking extraordinary steps to ensure his safety. I am sure you would agree, this is not an outcome that would benefit anyone."

We needed a break—this was exhausting. An hour sitting on the deck overlooking the lake and mountains, eating hamburgers, hotdogs, potato salad and chips, certainly brought the relaxation our bodies and minds craved. This is how work should be every day. Or better yet, I thought, this is how one should live in retirement. A brief walk down to the covered boat dock ended our break and we all returned to the same seats we occupied this morning.

Jim picked up the conversation with a discussion of the media. "The media has always been the fourth leg of democracy in this country," Jim began. "Unfortunately, we can no longer count on the mainstream media to fulfill that vital role. The press has let President Sanchez get away with untruth after untruth, never questioning opposing statements or wildly exaggerated statistics, or under reported unemployment rates and deficit figures. It reminds me of third world countries where the government controls the press. If it wasn't for talk radio and certain cable channels, the truth would never surface. Now the President is talking about bringing back the 'fairness doctrine' to silence all who oppose his policies. We cannot allow this to occur." Again, all responded, "Amen!"

Jim continued. "What we now must determine are their vulnerabilities. By this, I mean those weaknesses that will allow us to actually see the inner workings of the White House and determine who is making the decisions, exactly what the informal structure looks like, how it operates and whether it passes the test of constitutionality. We all know any activity outside their constitutional authority will be rooted in egotism, power and money. And the President and his senior staff are too arrogant not to make a mistake. We need to be in a position to recognize that mistake and take the appropriate action, to include perhaps, doing nothing, depending on the timing. Chuck, why don't you brief us as to what you have found out so far?"

"Let me start by stating that we can absolutely not trust my ASAC, Jeffrey Polk," I said emphatically, hoping that would get their full attention. "Polk was assigned to me about six weeks ago by the White House Chief of Staff Stewart Cohn, who happens to be the second person on my 'Do Not Trust List.' Both Polk and Cohn have lied to me a number of times and I have been put into a situation where Cohn ignores me and goes directly to Polk. I did not ignore it, but I did not make such a big deal of it that I could end up transferred out of the White House. Last week, Cohn directed Polk to allegedly discuss VIP security with the Mexican Embassy. Given the number of government officials being gunned down by the Mexican drug cartels, this would not be an unusual request. What was unusual was that no one told me about it until later, and when I checked, I found that Polk had not gone to the Embassy, but instead to the Mayflower Hotel on Connecticut Avenue. Once I got in touch with him on his cell phone, I ordered him to see me by the end of the day. Evidently, following my call to him, he called Cohn at his townhouse in Old Town Alexandria and then he called James Martino, the Hispanic Liaison Czar, who just happens to be a convicted felon. I have no idea what this is all about, but with Jim's assistance, we have video from the Mayflower which we will all review later." Jim smiled, nodding his head and holding up four discs.

"One other incident needs to be brought to your attention," I continued. "One night last June at about 9:30 p.m., I was returning to the White House with the President and noticed the West Wing lit up like a Christmas tree. The President noticed it as well, but never said a word. My agents tucked the President in and I went to Cohn's office to see what was going on. Inside Cohn's office were eight men. Four of them I recognized. Now I know the fifth was James Martino. I have no idea who the other three were, but I am working on it. These Thursday night meetings have continued, taking place at least once a month. I will likewise keep you up-to-date as more information develops."

Jim again stood up to speak once I was finished. "I think the best approach for the remainder of the day would be to review what we have from the Mayflower, courtesy of a retired FBI agent," Jim told the group. "As we review it, I will stop it if any one of you recognizes any individual and we will record the time and all we see. Once completed, it is time to go fishing with dinner being served at 7:30 p.m. Poker begins at 9:30 p.m.," Jim concluded. Everyone cheered!

The video was very clear and faces were easily recognizable throughout the lobby. There was a 5x zoom capability which allowed us to actually read the headlines on the newspapers lying on tables in the lobby. Jim had the video at a low speed that gave us all time to view each person as they entered or left the area. The audio was noisy as expected and my guess is that we would need some technical support to extract any individual conversations which we thought to be relevant. All and all, it was better than I expected. I am certain there are hundreds of private investigators that pay big bucks for video of this quality, especially from hotel lobbies.

The tape read 8:53 a.m. when Polk entered the hotel lobby. I asked Jim to stop the video as I explained who he was and reminded everyone what he had told me when I called him at 9:02 a.m. It just hit me that there was no logical reason for what we were seeing and the reality of the situation is that we are looking at a "dirty cop." He outright lied to me and in my mind, there was no other way to look at it.

Jim continued the video. Polk walked over to a chair and took a seat. He had nothing in his hand. Two minutes later, two men approached Polk. Again, the video was paused. The one on the left was unknown to any of us, probably Hispanic. He had a five-inch briefcase in his left hand. However, the one to the right was James Martino. He had a folder in his left hand. Introductions were made and there was a conversation that lasted a little less than two minutes. The unknown male held out his right hand to shake Polk's hand again, and at the same time handed him the briefcase. He then turned and shook Martino's hand and left the hotel. Polk and Martino then started a conversation.

Steve suddenly asked that the tape be stopped. He had noticed another Hispanic male get up from his chair in the lobby, lay his paper down on the lobby table, pick up what appeared be a small suitcase and exit the hotel about 15 seconds after the first Hispanic male had left. Polk handed Martino the briefcase and at the same time Martino gave Polk the folder he was holding, they shook hands and then at 9:00 a.m., Martino left the hotel. Polk went to a chair, sat down and opened the folder. From what we could see, the folder contained several pages stapled together. At exactly 9:02 a.m., Polk answered his cell phone. I had Jim stop the tape as I announced, "Perfect timing on my part," knowing that was the call I made to Polk. "The problem," Jim added, "is that Polk now thinks he could have been surveilled, and they will probably change locations. But, your timing was good." At 9:04 a.m. we could see Polk making the call to Cohn and at 9:10 a.m. making the call to Martino.

We went back to about 8:00 a.m. and started reviewing the video again. Martino came into the Hotel at 8:11 a.m. and went right to the elevator pushing the button for the fifth floor. He had nothing in his hands. We spent about another hour watching the videos, but no additional information was extracted.

"You all realize that I have enough evidence to formally charge ASAC Polk and see to it that he is terminated from the Secret Service," I told the group.

"But," Joe added, "now that we know him better than he thinks we do, we can use him to our advantage."

I added, "Exactly what I was thinking."

"My best guess is that the first unidentified Hispanic male stayed at the Mayflower last Tuesday night somewhere on the fifth floor," Jim stated. "It should not be a problem getting a list of all those who stayed on the fifth floor that evening."

"Let's pick this conversation up tomorrow morning." the General told the group. He concluded the work for the day by announcing "The beer is ice cold and the fish are waiting!" Again, everyone cheered. This spy business was starting to look very appealing.

I was the only one who did not catch a fish, but it made no difference. We all were delighted no matter who made the catch and ceremoniously released each one.

Dinner included grilled steaks, baked potatoes, salad, corn on the cob and rolls. Following dinner, we all went to the deck for an after dinner drink and ended our eating binge with strawberry cheesecake and coffee. Fortunately, the conversation turned to the usual men's topics—family, football and fishing. The poker game lasted to about 11:00 p.m. with no real losers or winners. It had been a good day, but we were all ready to call it a night.

SUNDAY, AUGUST 26

Late yesterday afternoon and last evening could not have been better. I know this is a guy thing, but we really got to know one another last night and truly bonded. There were no egos present, just six men who spent their lives in public service and love their country.

After a large buffet style breakfast, it was time to get back to work. We had an hour long discussion on what we saw in the videos yesterday afternoon, trying to determine what was going on inside the Mayflower Hotel. Our focus centered on what was passed in the briefcase. Drugs were ruled out and we settled on currency, some sort of confidential agreement or classified material—probably "secret" or "top secret." My assignment was to determine if that briefcase entered the White House, which should not be too difficult.

The remainder of the morning was consumed going over the names and backgrounds of everyone on the White House staff. I was shocked not only as to the large number, but how little information we knew about some key players. There is no doubt that formal security protocols have been violated, but by what authority? We already knew that the Chief of Staff was handling all the paperwork and security checks on the so called czars. That alone left a gaping hole in White House security. Now the question is, do I take this matter up the Secret Service chain of command? If the answer is "yes," how hard do I push? Do I risk a chance that I will be transferred off the White House Detail? If so, we lose our "inside spy," and that was not acceptable to me and hopefully not acceptable to the others.

After a lengthy discussion on White House security breaches, I suggested that I order ASAC Jeff Polk to make sure all security protocols are being followed. He is to complete the assignment informally, but in writing, without bending any noses out of joint and report back to me in two weeks. It will be interesting to see how he words that report.

The ride home seemed relatively short, probably because of

the discussion. The majority of the time was spent trying to come to a consensus as to who was calling the shots in the White House. Given the undisputed fact that the President was a narcissist, perhaps he is calling all the shots. Or is there an unknown confidant behind the scene.

As we pulled into the mall, it did not take us but a few seconds to realize we had a problem. "Don't stop," Joe yelled to Jim. "As we drive around, everybody, look at your own vehicle and assess the damage," Joe ordered. "And Jim, drive to the other side of the building so we can figure this out." Jim pulled the van into an area quite a distance from the areas where we had parked our cars on Saturday morning.

"We cannot be certain that someone is not waiting for us to return to our vehicles," Joe explained.

"OK, damage report," Jim began, "Judge?"

"Broken passenger window," he responded.

"General?"

"Broken driver's window," the General stated.

"Steve?"

"Broken passenger window also," said Steve.

"Chuck?" Jim concluded.

"No apparent damage that I could see," I answered.

"We need to pick up the cars without a lot of fanfare, so you need to walk through the mall and pick up your cars and anything on the ground around your car," Joe instructed. "There could be a bug in your car, so do not say anything and do not use your cell phone. Obviously, we are not going to report this to the Arlington County Police since it will link us together. We will meet in 15 minutes at the intersection of 16th Street South and South Ives Street adjacent to Virginia Highlands Park. When you get there, check and see what is missing from your vehicle. I will then scan each car for any electronic bugs and then we can all head for home. Remember check for tails both here and on the way home," Joe concluded.

It took less than 15 minutes to reassemble. After looking at each car, Joe could not determine what was used to break the car windows. While there was glass on the seats of the cars, there were no rocks or evidence of any other projectile. Nothing was missing from any of the vehicles and if any owner information was copied from the registration or insurance identification card, it was not apparent. Joe scanned all the vehicles with negative results. Maybe it was just kids smashing car windows, but we couldn't be sure.

Steve shared that his nephew worked as a patrol officer for Arlington PD and he offered to call him to see how many similar cases occurred in the area this weekend.

"Let's hold off on that for now," Joe suggested. "Give me a few days and let me see what I can find out. I can at least find out if any of your registration tags were run through the Department of Motor Vehicles." We all agreed.

Jim added, "I also believe it would be prudent for all of us to start taking extra precautions in everything we do. Make sure you continue to check for tails wherever you go. Note any strange cars in your neighborhoods. Do not let anyone you do not absolutely trust into your homes, and it's time to tell your families that as well. You have all been through this before. Remember, Joe will be calling you this week to schedule an electronic scan for any audio or visual surveillance devices in or near your homes. It would be best if your family is not at home."

"How much do we tell our families?" Steve asked Jim.

"For now," Jim replied, "just tell them there have been

unconfirmed threats on unspecified individuals and everyone involved in any aspect of law enforcement should take extra precautions. If there are no more questions, thank you for all your work this weekend; we are well into our mission. Good luck and Godspeed."

"Freedom prospers when religion is vibrant and the rule of law under God is acknowledged."
—Thomas Jefferson

CHAPTER 6

MONDAY, AUGUST 27

Again I did not sleep very well last night. Why were all the cars broken into except my daughter's—the one I was driving? I just do not think it was a random act of vandalism. Nothing appeared to be missing from any of the vehicles. Is someone watching us or watching me? If it was me, am I responsible for giving up our entire group? If that is true, we now have to take measures to safeguard our families. Maybe I am just being paranoid; after all, I am new to this double agent/spy business. I do not know how those men and women do this type of work day after day!

It hit me like a ton of bricks as soon as I walked into my office. Cohn had ordered my move to this office. I immediately felt sick to my stomach and broke out into a sweat. I could not wait any longer, I had to find out.

It was now 7:10 a.m. I had about an hour at the very most. I looked up the number and dialed it as fast as possible using my covert cell phone. I then immediately stepped out of my office into the reception area which was unoccupied until about 8:15 a.m.

"Technical Support Services, Oates," Steve said as he answered the phone.

"Steve, this is Chuck Burke, I need you to come over to my office, right away and sweep my office for any bugs, are you available?"

"For you I am, but we did the entire West Wing last week," Steve replied.

"They moved my office last month," I told him. "I will explain when you get here. And Steve, no one is to know, so how long will it take you to get here?"

"Twenty minutes and I am on my way," Steve said proudly.

"I will meet you at the east service entrance," I said before hanging up the phone. After years of working surveillance, Steve could maneuver a car through the Washington traffic better than any human being on earth. The 20 minute trip for Steve would take anyone else 30 minutes.

Eighteen minutes later, Steve and I were walking down the hallway to my office. Once inside, he looked around and whispered, "Who did you piss off?"

I motioned for Steve to step outside the office. "Long story, but Cohn wanted my office for one of the President's czars," I told him. "Or he wanted me out of the way," I added. "There isn't time to do a full sweep, but you have 30 minutes now and you can come back this evening to finish up. I hope that works for you."

"No problem," Steve said as he opened his bag of electronic equipment and got to work. He started in the far corner of my office covering the walls rather quickly. He spent much more time with the furniture and furnishings, but the majority of his available time was spent around my desk. Twenty minutes later, he had two listening devices in evidence bags.

Steve said quietly, "The first one was attached to the wall clock and captured any conversations in the room. The second one was on the underside of the bottom drawer of your desk, probably used to capture your end of the conversation during phone calls. Both are wireless transmitters and the receiver would have to be within 500 to 600 feet of your office. I want to look at them further and I will need to come back this evening to do a complete scan. Thanks for not hanging anything else on your walls; that made my job much easier."

In a low voice, I thanked him and walked him back to the east service door to exit the White House.

In less than an hour, my life has been turned upside down. And now it wasn't only my life, but the lives of my five partners and all our families. Lord knows I cannot speak freely in my office, the car could be bugged as well and I do not even want to think about my home. I went back to my office, locked it up for all the good that does and headed down the street where I could make some urgent calls that were about to change a lot of lives. I really did not expect an "Oh shit" of this magnitude so early in our assignment. How could I have been that stupid? My frustration of months had now turned to anger.

I ended up in the lobby of the J. W. Marriott on 14th and Pennsylvania Avenue. Using my generic cell phone, my first call went to Jim. After explaining all that had happened in the last hour and a half, Jim's only words were, "Let me think about this for a few minutes and I will call you back." Not exactly words of comfort.

My next call went to my wife from my regular cell phone. "Kim," I said, "How about meeting me for an early dinner this afternoon after work?"

"This is a bit unusual, what's up? Is everything OK?" was her reply.

"Everything is fine," I lied, "I just thought we would do something different for a change. I will meet you at Jonathan's at 5:00 if that works for you."

There was a short silence and then Kim responded, "I have a couple of errands to run so that works for me. See you at five."

Jonathan's was a neighborhood restaurant about two miles from our home. I knew that I had some explaining to do; Kim was too bright not to know something was up. Quite honestly, I did not want her walking into the house alone until I figured out the necessary precautionary steps. How much I am going to tell her probably depends on what occurs over the next eight hours.

Jim called back in exactly ten minutes. That was one characteristic I truly admired. When Jim told you anything, and I mean anything, you could count on it!

"Chuck, hear me out and then we can discuss some options," Jim began. "Joe Wells is on his way to your home to do a thorough security check. If he needs keys he will call you, but that probably won't be necessary." That was not reassuring, I thought. Jim continued, "Today's discovery has dramatically changed the game plan. I am not sure how much they now know, but let's assume that it is quite extensive. We do know that once they find the listening devices have been removed from your office, their game plan will change as well. They will not confront you for fear you will go public with everything you know. To our advantage, they have no idea what we know at this time. You and I are now going to continue our mission overtly, leaving the other four to continue their work covertly for now. My thought is that they will monitor the two of us very closely so we will need to have a well-defined strategy in order to use this as an opportunity. Both our families are now in danger and setting up protection for them will be my first priority. Second, I will figure a way for the six of us to meet as soon as possible. What you need to do is go back to the office and pretend it is just another normal day. I know that will be difficult, but it is extremely important that you continue as if nothing has gone wrong. Understand?"

"I understand, Jim," I said, not really meaning it, "but I am worried about our families. I called Kim to meet her for an early dinner because I did not want her alone in the house until I could be assured of her safety. And remember, my daughter is at William and Mary and my son is at James Madison University."

"I will take responsibility for the safety of our families," Jim stated, "and trust me on this. Nothing will happen to them. Let me get started on all of this. Call me back at about four o'clock from a secure location." And with that, the call ended.

I walked back to my office and exchanged pleasantries with the office staff before closing my door, which was nothing out of the ordinary. I sat at my desk and my mind went in a hundred different directions. Think about it. Here I am working in the White House—the home of the most powerful man in the free world, the center of democracy, where the most important decisions are made, and the most secure building in America, if not the world. Yet, I did not feel safe and secure from within. If there is ever a time for God to bless America, it is right now. All morning long, I sat in my office waiting for the hammer to drop. Would I be summoned to Cohn's office? Would Secret Service Headquarters notify me of a change in assignment to get me out of the White House? How would I handle my first conversation with ASAC Polk? How loyal is the remainder of my staff? How many people really know what is going on here? Many questions, but no answers.

The highlight of my day thus far was a call from Joe Wells. His message was short, "Call me when you can talk." I told the staff I was going to lunch, although food was the furthest thing from my mind. Five minutes later I had Joe on the phone.

"What's up?" I asked. None of the normal 'Hi, how are you' or anything close; this was pure business.

Joe explained the situation very briefly. "Your home is safe and secure. There are two small gadgets in the left kitchen cabinet that look like remote garage door openers. One has a single emergency button that sends a silent alarm. This is for your wife. The second has two buttons— the emergency button and a second button for scanning for listening devices. When you press it and a green light comes on, talk freely. If the red light comes on, there is a listening device in range and any talk should be guarded. If you or your wife press the emergency button twice, and it has to be twice, you will have help in less than one minute. I will do all your vehicles tonight. Leave them in the driveway. Talk to you soon."

The one-sided conversation with Joe made me feel a little better. Explaining all of this to my wife would be difficult, at best. What do I say to make her more aware of her surroundings, more cautious and more alert, yet not so paranoid or scared that she acts unnatural to everyone she knows? I felt a surge of anger that I and my colleagues who've taken the oath to protect our country have to subject our families to these dangers.

Four o'clock could not come soon enough and it was finally here. I had already left the White House and was heading south on 14th Street to get to Interstate 95 toward my home and Jonathan's Restaurant. As usual, traffic was moving slow and I was concentrating on what I was going to say to Kim. The honk of a horn got my attention and as I looked to my left, I saw a Hispanic male in a car going in the opposite direction on 14th Street. He looked right at me and with his index finger and thumb extended to simulate a handgun, he pointed to me and raised his arm twice, indicating two shots fired. What in the hell was that? A threat? A scare tactic? Or was it totally unrelated to what I was doing? I am not certain, but he certainly looked like the unidentified Hispanic male in the Mayflower. Whatever the case, I definitely need to pay closer attention to my surroundings.

I was not certain if it was safe to talk in my car, so I exited 95, pulled into a gas station and walked far enough away from my vehicle to ensure a private conversation from my cell phone.

"Jim," I said as soon as the phone was answered.

"You doing OK, Chuck?" was Jim's reply.

"For the time being," I answered, "but I certainly got us into a hell of a mess."

"Not your fault," Jim said in a calm voice. "I am sure Joe told you about everything that he has done. Your wife, son and daughter are being protected by the best and your home is being watched 24 hours a day. In fact, we all have security. I will give everyone a detailed explanation as soon as we meet. Be at my house at 9:30 this evening. Do not worry about any tails; just drive over and come to the front door. The light will be on for you." And with that, he hung up the phone.

I got back in my car and again headed south on Interstate 95. With the 14th Street incident clearly on my mind, I drove like a maniac for about five minutes, weaving in and out of traffic, changing lanes and speeding the best I could through the heavy traffic. I am certain other motorists were calling 911 about my reckless driving, but my license plates were confidential and a check with DMV would return a "not on file." Once I was certain that I was not being followed, I once again became that safe, courteous driver I have always been. Then I started thinking. I was really hoping the call to Jim would make me feel better, but that definitely was not the case. In fact, I felt sick to my stomach. This is all getting too weird, even for me, and there was nothing I could do about it.

Dinner with Kim was uncomfortable for both of us. Kim knew something was up but knew enough not to bring it up in the restaurant. Now knowing our home did not contain any listening devices, I also thought it best if we waited until we got home. I was nervous for I knew I was about to end her naive view of the world, something I never wanted to do. Somehow, I think she knew that as well. We ate quietly, but faster than we normally do, probably because of nerves. Kim asked if I had spoken to the kids since they returned to college. It was apparent she suspected something and knowing Kim, she was certainly hoping that whatever it is, it would not affect Tom and Marie.

Too late, I thought. "No, I haven't spoken to either one of them since they left," I said, "but let's give them a call later this evening."

We were home by six o'clock and sitting at the kitchen table, both apprehensive about the conversation that was about to take place. Everyone in law enforcement has had nightmares about this exact moment. Not one of us wants to drag our family into the chaotic, unexplainable and sometimes unbelievable reality of the real world of good guys versus bad guys. We see it all change, from the best man has to give, to the worst of man's inhumane treatment of the human race. But here I was, in the exact the position I prayed I would never be.

I started by telling Kim how important family is to me, something she already knew. Instead of calming her anxieties, she started to look pale and I knew I needed to get right to the point. I quickly stated everything would be fine and then told Kim everything. I had to, my world was becoming smaller and smaller. There were only a few people left that I absolutely trusted. Kim was on the top of the list. She began to tremble, first her lips, then her hands. Next the tears started with periods of crying and disbelief. And last came the hard questions. Are you sure we are going to be all right? Are the kids safe? What do I need to do? Do we need to go into hiding? Are we safe in our own home? And then the question we all have been asking—what is happening to our country?

We moved to the living room sofa where I held her in my arms for the next hour. There was not one stone left unturned and that is the way it should be. My job has destroyed the naivety of my family and the outcome will surely have an effect on how we live the rest of our lives and most likely the country's future. But the alternative of doing absolutely nothing would certainly destroy all hope of a continuation of our lifestyle as we now know it.

We decided to call the kids together at about 8:00 p.m. in hopes that they would be in their room studying. Together we decided not to tell them anything about our earlier conversation until Jim gave me some more details on how they were being protected. Tom received the first call. He was at the local pub having a pizza with several of his friends. Everything was going fine with him and he was in a rush to get us off the phone, stating he would give us a call later. When we called Marie, she was at the gym working out "with Ted" who was her trainer. Likewise, she told us she could not talk right now, but would call us after she and Ted "grabbed a salad" after their workout.

"So much for academics," I said to Kim upon hanging up the phone.

She laughed for the first time this evening and offered, "It is comforting to know they have always been good students, or I would think we are wasting a lot of money in an attempt to educate our children."

"My job," I stated, "is to call each of them from Jim's once I learn how they are being protected. Your job is to get the low down on Ted!"

"Honey," Kim responded, "your little girl is all grown up or she certainly will be after you talk to her later this evening. While I love how protective you are, I worry that all of this will change her and take some of the joy out of life at a time when she is truly gaining her independence and self-assurance. I do not think she is naïve; she is spirited, trusting and fun loving. I do not want her to change. Tom, on the other hand, will look at this as an adventure and I would like to see him take something more serious for once.

Do you understand what I am trying to say?"

"I understand completely," I reassured Kim, "but I worry about you more than the kids. I can only promise that I will do whatever it takes to keep all of you safe from any harm."

"... if one advances confidently in the direction of his dreams and endeavors to live a life which he has imagined, he will meet with a success unexpected in common hours. He will put something behind and will pass an invisible boundary."
—Henry David Thoreau

CHAPTER 7

After the difficult conversation with my wife and all that was on my mind, I really do not remember much about the 40 minute trip to Jim's house. I did however, vigilantly check for tails. I was quite sure that there were none. I figured Cohn and his cronies were probably having a meeting of their own.

The light was on and I walked directly to the front door and rang the bell. Jim opened the door with his usual smile, which given all that has taken place, rather surprised me. Again, I was the last one to arrive even though I was five minutes early. The next time, I will be 30 minutes early!

After the usual hand shaking with the others, I asked Jim

how Patricia, his wife, was accepting all this. "She's a champ at this stuff," Jim told me. "In fact, while you were on your way here, she called Kim and they are probably having coffee together right now," he continued while glancing at his watch. All I could say is, "Thanks," and Jim just smiled again.

"OK, time to get down to business," Jim started. "Most importantly, Joe has already checked this house, and it is clear, so talk freely. In fact, Joe has been busy today and has cleared all your homes as well."

"And tonight, I will clear all your vehicles, so leave them in the driveway locked," Joe added.

"How about keys?" asked Steve.

"Don't need them."

Jim spoke again, this time without a smile on his face. "The first and most important topic of this evening is about safety— ours and our families. I am sure most of you are familiar with the private security group, WATCH24. This group hires only the best and has been used extensively throughout the country and many of the troubled parts of the world, to include the Middle East. What you do not know is that I am a silent partner and have been involved with WATCH24 since my retirement from the FBI. WATCH24 has been assigned to protect each of you and your immediate families. You will never see them or know they are close by, but trust me, this is their primary assignment, and they have your backs covered. Each member of your family has or will have a wireless electronic device that will 'bring out the cavalry' if the button is pressed twice. In addition, your six individual devices will enable you to check for any electronic eavesdropping devices in your vicinity with the mere press of a second button."

Jim continued, "Right now, I would like for Chuck and Steve to call their children at college and explain that an unsubstantiated, generic threat has been made against you and as an extra precaution, an agent will be in touch with them in 30 minutes. And explain to them they will have a personal alarm for their safety should they need it. And finally, it goes without saying that they are not to mention this to anyone. So, let's take ten. Patricia left us coffee and cookies in the kitchen."

Both Tom and Marie were understanding and appeared to be extremely calm as I relayed the script that Jim suggested. Marie jokingly asked if she could change her last name. Tom stated that he, being the "big brother," would check on Marie regularly.

With coffee and cookies in hand, we reconvened in the family room and Jim continued where he left off. "All aspects of the protection plan are now in place," he announced, "and now let's talk strategy." And all at once Jim was smiling again. Jim explained in detail the discovery of the two electronic eavesdropping devices in my office earlier today. I added that Steve Oates would be returning this evening to my office to complete the search.

Still smiling, Jim went on. "The recent events have certainly changed our game plan, but I see this as an opportunity rather than a problem. Joe tells me that our vehicles were the only ones damaged in the mall parking lot. Given what we now know, that is understandable. But what I find more interesting is what the General has to report."

With that, General Monroe stood up and started speaking. "As you know, President Sanchez has cut the number of Border Patrol agents working the southern border, cut the number of DEA agents working the Mexican drug cartel cases and has canceled the

Executive Order that permitted the National Guard to assist the Border Patrol. Needless to say, intelligence sources have indicated a substantial increase in the quantity of drugs entering the United States through the Mexican Border. What are more troubling are the intelligence reports indicating that al-Qaida and the Iran-backed terrorist group Hezbollah are working with the Mexican Drug Cartels to smuggle terrorists and nuclear material across the border as well. All indications are that al-Qaida now has enough material in the United States for five to ten dirty bombs. I need not tell you what this would do to our country. President Sanchez and others have been advised of this, but to date no additional preventive action has been taken. In fact, rumor has it that the President is about to appoint another czar to oversee border security thereby usurping all the responsibility and authority now vested in a number of federal agencies—the Border Patrol, the FBI, the CIA and the Department of Homeland Defense, to name a few.

"What does the President have to gain from this failure to take action? First, there is some indication that large sums of money are being paid to certain members of the White House senior staff. Chuck, that briefcase at the Mayflower may have been part of that transfer. Some trusted members of the CIA are still trying to identify the two unknowns who were involved in that transaction. The second reason is even more troubling. President Sanchez may be allowing these actions to assist in implementing some of his unpopular priorities as "Emergency Executive Orders" to include registration and/or confiscation of personal firearms, creation of a national protection agency to replace law enforcement, and eventually the military, and control of the industrial markets and the banks. I think you could imagine the panic that would be widespread in America if a few dirty bombs exploded in the country. The public would demand immediate action by the federal government. Once he has his agenda in place, the President would tighten up the borders and bring peace and calm to America. He would most likely regain the trust of the country, reassuring his reelection. In my opinion, it's all about retaining and strengthening his power."

The General sat down, and Jim stood up. He said nothing and the room remained silent. Knowing Jim as I do, this was probably intentional so what the General just told us could sink in.

Finally, Jim smiled and asked, "Does anyone see any opportunity here? Well, I do. Let me begin by telling you that Stewart Cohn, Jeffrey Polk and James Martino are all under 24-hour surveillance by WATCH24. Chuck, obviously we cannot monitor their activities in the White House, but I think I have a solution to that as well. We will now have two distinctive operations—one overt and one covert. Chuck, as I shared with you earlier today, you and I are now out in the open. They already know about us and we are going to make them think we know much more than we actually do. The remainder of you will remain behind the scenes in your covert status.

Steve, I want you to start preparing the affidavits for electronic intercepts for Cohn, Polk and Martino. Let me know if you have any holes that need to be filled. General, that was an excellent report. Please continue to keep us up-to-date. Judge, give us a week or so and we will be asking for some court orders. Joe, please start researching which cell and landline phones Cohn, Polk and Martino use regularly. Chuck, could you arrange it so I could stop by and visit you in your office in the White House tomorrow?"

"Sure," I replied, "as long as it is after noon."

"Let's say 1:00 p.m., I want to make sure you introduce me to Polk when he is back from lunch," Jim said with a smile larger than ever. "One more thing before we all start home," Jim concluded. "Be available on your cell every evening at 5:55 p.m. for daily updates." And with that, the meeting was over.

The first thing I did on the drive home was to again call my kids and reassure them everything was fine. They seemed to accept it almost like it is just a part of life when your father is in law enforcement. Just hearing their calm voices gave me some relief. I was relieved by the protection my family was receiving, but apprehensive about their future. I was scared for our country, but hopeful we could make a difference. And I was thankful to God for bringing us this far and I trusted Him to make it all right.

As soon as I walked in the door, I saw Kim sitting at the kitchen table and knew something was up. "Sit down," she said, "we need to talk."

"Patricia told me something tonight that shocked me and surely will shock you as well. She told me that she is planning to leave Jim and move in with their daughter in Detroit. After all the years Jim spent in the FBI, and her worrying about him every time he was late or out on a special assignment, she was holding on for his retirement thinking it would all change. Now she knows that nothing has changed, and she can't do it anymore. She loves Jim, but all the worry is taking a toll on her health and she sees no other solution. Once she leaves the house, she is hoping Jim will really retire and if he does, she will come home."

"You are right, I am shocked," I replied. "Tonight, when I asked him how Patricia was accepting all this, he told me 'she's a champ at this.' This will crush him. Does Jim have any idea that Patricia is about to leave him?

"No," Kim said, "and she told me in confidence and that she did not want me to tell you. So you can't say a word to Jim. What should we do?"

"I don't know. But maybe I will tell him to thank Patricia again for coming over here tonight and see if I can start a dialogue about all that our wives have to deal with in this business."

"All tyranny needs to gain a foothold is for people of good conscience to remain silent."
—Thomas Jefferson

CHAPTER 8

TUESDAY, AUGUST 28

My home phone rang at 3:10 a.m., which was not a regular occurrence. Half asleep, I answered it quickly hoping it would not wake Kim. "Burke," I said and waited for a response.

"Boss, this is Bob Smith," replied one of the Secret Service agents assigned to the White House. "I just got a call from the Washington Field Office. One of our agents was shot and killed last night in an apparent robbery attempt while he was going from his car to his home. It happened in Rockville, and we are on the scene working with the local police."

Needless to say, I was sitting up in bed now, wide awake. "Do you have a name, Bob?" I asked.

"Steve Oates, from the Technical Unit," he responded.

I was in shock. My chest started pounding and I could barely say "Thank you" before I hung up the phone.

"Those dirty bastards," I yelled, startling my wife.

"What's wrong?" she said in a relatively calm voice.

"They shot and killed Steve Oates," I said through my tears. She reached over and held me, both of us lying there as the tears were mounting. I cannot begin to tell you the guilt I felt.

Jim picked up his cell phone on the first ring. I basically repeated what the White House duty agent had relayed to me, reminding Jim that Steve was working last night to finish the sweep of my office.

"Robbery, hell," was Jim's response. "This means that we need to step up our investigation immediately. See you at your office at one o'clock. And Chuck, I am sorry. I know you and Steve were good friends. I will take care of notifying the rest of our crew.

I had to go to the scene. There is no way to deny it. I was largely responsible for Agent Oates' death. I was convinced that if I had not given him the White House assignment, he would still be alive. I held out my badge as I approached the police perimeter and was waved through by one of the local officers. I parked about 25 yards from the crime tape and got out of my car. A Rockville Police Captain immediately came up to me and escorted me into the crime scene. Steve was lying there on the pavement covered by a bloody sheet. Without hesitation, the forensic technician pulled the sheet off his body. With one shot to the chest and one shot through his head, most likely the second shot by the murderer to ensure death, Steve never stood a chance. His weapon was still in his holster on his belt. There was little doubt in my mind that this was an outright hit and not a robbery gone badly.

I spent some time at the scene command post reviewing the facts of the case with the Rockville Deputy Chief and Bob Wilson, the Secret Service Special Agent-in-Charge of the Washington Field Office. I had to tell Bob, in confidence, that Agent Oates had just completed a special assignment for me at the White House and that if any additional information was needed, I would be the contact. So far, there were several witnesses that heard the shots, but no worthwhile description of the perpetrator or perpetrators.

I left the scene and headed to the White House once it became apparent that my staying served no real purpose. I spent the time driving going over all the "what ifs." I can't begin to tell you the pain I was feeling. Gradually, the pain turned to more anger and surprisingly less fear. It now seemed all very clear to me as to what I now had to do. I was not only ready, I was anxious.

Walking into the White House, it was obvious we had lost one of our brothers. All the agents were courteous, but not one had a smile on his or her face. I knew the next several days would be difficult for all of us; it always is. Steve had been married once, years ago, but it did not last very long. As far as I knew, they did not have any children. He was originally from upstate New York where he began his law enforcement career in the State Police. If I remember correctly, he came to the Secret Service in the early eighties. He loved doing all the technical work and he was damn good at what he did.

I walked into my office knowing that Steve had been there just hours earlier. I sat at my desk and first said a prayer for both of us—that he would enjoy his everlasting life and that mine would come much later, for I had much more work to do in this world.

I opened my desk drawer and saw the note from Steve. I carefully took it out and read it:

Chuck

I checked over your entire office very carefully and you are good to go for now. I would suggest that I do this at least once a week until you think it is no longer necessary. Attached is an evidence bag containing the two devices I removed earlier today. Both of these are easily purchased in a number of stores throughout the country. Oddly enough, they are not available in the Washington Metro area, but can be mail ordered from New York or Miami. I have additional information in my formal report. For obvious reasons, I will mail you all copies of the report to your home and you should have it tomorrow. Thanks for including me and keep me posted

Take care,

Steve

"And you take care of yourself, my friend," I said aloud. I took the note and the evidence bag containing the listening devices and placed them in a large plain envelope and wrote "James W. Bruce" on the outside, dated it with the time, initialed it and sealed it with tape.

I then called the Special Agent-in-Charge of the Washington Field Office to see if there was any additional information on the shooting. He did tell me that Steve never got his weapon out of his holster and that he believed it was not a robbery as reported by the local police. His wallet was missing, but his badge, credentials, money clip and weapon looked as if they were not touched. "Perhaps someone wanted it to look like a robbery," I stated, trying to plant the seed. He agreed and told me he was going to pursue it from that angle.

The rest of the morning was spent doing nothing official. I called Kim to see how she was doing. She was just as concerned about me as I was about her. I called both my children and checked on them. They were both going along, happy as ever, not realizing the severity of the situation. That was a relief. I walked around the office twice, looking for what I do not know. Then I sat and carefully plotted a game plan for the next few days. I spent more than half that time rehearsing how I would respond when I was called to Cohn's office to tell me I was being transferred off the White House Detail.

Jim, being as punctual as always, was at the White House at exactly one o'clock. I walked out to meet him since he had to be escorted and we both returned to my office.

"I have had a busy morning," he began. "I met with Steve this morning and told him I need Title III orders to intercept the phones of Cohn, Polk and Martinez, and I needed them signed by the Judge by the end of the day. Joe is working on the technical end of it so we waste no time getting it completed. I had the Judge swear in five retired FBI agents who happen to work for WATCH24. I was sworn in as well. The five will be monitoring the calls once the orders are signed. Is there anything we can do with the White House phones?" Jim was asking me.

"I thought about that," I said, "but the only solution I could come up with is to tell Cohn that there are a number of unsubstantiated threats against the President's senior staff and we would be monitoring incoming and outgoing calls. This is not that unusual."

"Good," Jim stated, "this will force them to use their home and cell phones. Now let's talk about our role. We need to make Cohn and Polk believe we know much more than we actually do in hopes they will make that one mistake that seals their fate. That is going to put a lot of pressure on you and perhaps cause your transfer out of the White House."

"I have thought about that possibility and trust me, I have my own game plan," I said confidently.

"I knew you would," Jim said proudly. "Now let the mind games begin. Why don't you call Polk to your office so I can meet him?"

In less than five minutes, Polk was knocking on my door. As he opened it, I motioned him in and stated, "Jeff, I thought it would be good for you to meet Jim Bruce, retired Deputy Director of the FBI and a good friend of the Secret Service."

The look on Polk's face revealed how uncomfortable this was for him. However, he went through the motions and stuck out his hand stating, "Jeff Polk, glad to meet you."

Jim was quick to respond, "Sit down Jeff, and let's talk for a few minutes." Polk reluctantly sat down in the chair next to Jim. He was getting more nervous and it was showing. Jim was not about to let up.

"So, Chuck tells me your last assignment was in El Paso," Jim began smiling. "Those Mexican Drug Cartels are raising hell down there. I have heard that they are now extorting money from El Paso businesses by threatening the death of family members. Did you have any contact with the cartels while you were in El Paso?"

"Not really," Jeff answered, "I am sure some of the other agents in the office had some cases involving the Mexican drug dealers, but I mostly did counterfeiting cases and VIP protection."

"You must have been good at it, to go from the El Paso Field Office to Assistant Agent-in-Charge at the White House," said

Jim, not letting Polk up for air.

"I guess I was just fortunate to be in the right place at the right time."

Jim continued, "You must speak fluent Spanish."

"I do," said Polk.

"Well, Jeff, you probably have some work to do, so I won't keep you. Why don't the three of us get together for lunch some day?" Jim said to close the conversation.

"That sounds good," Polk said as he stood up and started toward the door.

"The Mayflower," Jim said loudly, stopping Polk in his tracts, "Have you ever had lunch in the Mayflower Hotel?"

Polk turned, his face as white as a ghost, and said, "No."

"Then that is where we will have lunch," Jim said as Polk walked out the door.

"Well, you certainly ruined his day," I told Jim.

"Not nearly as much as he has wrecked ours! However, we have only just begun." I opened my desk drawer and gave Jim what Steve Oates had left me last night before his death. "More evidence," I said. "Open it and read the note."

It was obvious to me that Jim had read it at least twice and he sat there looking down, deep in thought. He finally looked up and stated, "Chuck, I think it is time to take another calculated risk and expand our base. I trust Tom Wilson, the FBI Deputy Director who took my position after I retired. This investigation obviously has far reaching tentacles which are beyond our capabilities. I am going from here to FBI Headquarters to feel him out. I will keep you posted. Also, in light of Steve's death, we need another meeting of our group. Since we have a contact at the Mayflower

Hotel and no one from the Administration would even consider going near the place, I will get a room and set up a private lunch for noon on Friday. Does that work for you?"

I responded without hesitation, "I'll make it work."

I escorted Jim out of the White House and returned to my office. I locked my door and spent the remainder of the day reviewing security records and recordings in search of the Mayflower briefcase to determine if it had entered the White House. After hours of searching, I found nothing. Perhaps it will appear on Thursday evening at the Chief of Staff's private meeting, I thought. In any case, I had planned to work a long day on Thursday using the evening hours to fulfill my responsibilities as a spy.

Kim and I had a nice dinner and spent the early evening discussing our retirement. It is not the first time the subject has come up, but it was the first time we got serious about it and gave it some direction. We definitely wanted out of the Washington Metro area and decided that we would go south. And we agreed that we needed to be on or near water. Our focus spanned the area from Virginia to Florida, and Kim said she would start searching the internet and create a list of possibilities. If nothing else, the conversation was a great diversion from the realities that were staring us in the face. I thought romance was out of the question after all that happened today. Later that evening, Kim proved me wrong.

WEDNESDAY, AUGUST 29

I drove to work this morning fully aware of my surroundings. My mind did wander for a brief period with the thought of Steve dying in that parking lot, alone and evidently never seeing his attacker. I certainly underestimated what the White House would do to retain their power. Jim was right. We needed more resources.

I really did not want to see Polk today and chances were he most likely did not want to see me. Hopefully his nerves were working overtime and he was beginning to feel uncomfortable in his own skin. When all this breaks wide open, I want to be part of the team that interrogates Polk. For whatever reason, I believe he would fold in less than ten minutes.

After an hour of searching for her telephone number, I called Steve Oates' sister to convey my condolences. She told me the family had decided on a private graveside service in upstate New York. However, she stated that after a request by the Secret Service, the family has agreed to a Memorial Service in Washington on Thursday morning at 10:00 a.m. I gave her my home and cell numbers and asked that I be called should she or any member of Steve's family need any assistance in the days ahead.

The official notice of the memorial service came out at 11:00 a.m. For whatever reason, actually seeing it in print hit me quite hard. I suddenly needed to get out of my office, out of the White House. I walked out with no real destination, but headed in the direction of the mall. I have always felt patriotic and at peace strolling among the monuments and memorials. It was a beautiful day with a rare break in the humidity for August. I have spent the majority of my career in and around Washington DC. After all these years, I still find it a wonderful and exciting place to be, in spite of President Sanchez and all his dealings. While leaving the area after retirement would not be difficult, I imagine that we will be traveling to our nation's capital at least twice a year, if for nothing else, to visit some of the sincere friends we made over the years.

I just now realized that I have picked up a tail. They already killed Steve; was I next? I have got to start paying closer attention to my surroundings. If this is a test on my observation abilities, I have again failed. I made a quick turn toward the Smithsonian. He walked past where I had turned, but eventually turned to the left as well. I quickly crossed 14th Street and started heading toward the Washington Monument. I walked for about three minutes before I looked back. It could have been my imagination, for he was nowhere in sight. I stopped by one of the street vendors and had what I refer to as the "dichotomous lunch"—a loaded hot dog with a diet soda. I took the time to take a full scan of my surroundings. He was nowhere to be seen. I sat on a bench for about five minutes and still no sight of him.

Feeling more relaxed, I headed up 15th Street toward the White House. I looked over my shoulder; damn, there he was again about a block behind me. Certainly he was not about to execute me in broad daylight on one of the busiest streets of the city. I made a sudden turn onto Pennsylvania Avenue toward the Capitol. With a quick glance, I saw him make the turn as well. I started walking slowly realizing my fear was again turning to anger. I took my weapon out of my holster and placed it in my suit coat pocket, leaving my hand there as well. I spun around and walked as fast as I could without running, directly toward him not knowing what to expect, but ready for anything.

When I was five feet from him, he spoke, "Good afternoon Mr. Burke, WATCH24, I've got your back."

The only audible word I could utter was a meek "Thanks." Now I don't know if I passed this test or failed it miserably. In my mind, I knew one thing. This spy stuff absolutely sucks.

The remaining afternoon hours were slow and I accomplished absolutely nothing. I actually spent some time daydreaming about retirement and a simpler life without all this stress.

Five o'clock finally came and I had started cleaning my desk to leave, when my group phone rang. As soon as I answered, Jim started talking, "It has been a very successful afternoon. We now have some help from the FBI, the court orders are moving forward, we should be up and running by tomorrow afternoon and the lunch for Friday is confirmed. Would it be all right if I went to Steve's memorial service with you tomorrow?"

"Sure," I answered, "it does sound like you had a very productive afternoon."

"More than you know. I will call you in the office in the morning," Jim said ready to hang up.

I quickly added, "Jim, thanks for covering my back." He laughed slightly and hung up.

I guess I will never know if I passed or failed this test, unless life itself is the defining answer.

"The wise man must remember that while he is a descendant of the past, he is a parent of the future."
—Herbert Spencer

CHAPTER 9

THURSDAY, AUGUST 30

I guess it was appropriate that it was raining today. The memorial service for Steve was much better attended than I expected. With more than a thousand people attending in a church that seats 500, Jim and I were fortunate to be seated in the fifth row, along with other bosses from the Secret Service. Sitting next to the Director of the Secret Service in the front row was Vice President Whitmore. When I brought that to Jim's attention, his only comment after some thought, was, "Interesting." Assistant Special Agent Jeffrey Polk would not be in attendance today since I ordered him to "hold down the fort" at the White House. The thought of him attending Steve's memorial service made me sick to my stomach, and besides I owed it to Steve to keep the enemy at a distance.

Both Jim and I had an opportunity to meet with Steve's family prior to the service. It is not easy to explain how difficult this is, unless you have been there. The reality of death is always at its peak when you first face the family. I never want to do this again and it is my prayer that this will be the last law enforcement funeral in my career. Steve's death was totally unnecessary. I knew that, but evidently Cohn and Polk did not feel they could take the chance. Where does that leave the six of us? Given our sudden overt role, I would think Jim and I must be on the top of their list.

In honor of Steve, the service was very well done. It was heartwarming and sincere, yet had a touch of humor that Steve would have enjoyed. He was the best at what he did, but those of us who spent significant time with him, appreciated his quick wit, sense of humor, and his never ending positive attitude.

Jim and I grabbed lunch after the service. According to him, the Judge was to sign the telephone intercept orders this morning. Joe was receiving some "unofficial" technical assistance from the FBI thanks to Deputy Director Tom Wilson, and everything should be operational by early afternoon. We spent some time discussing the plans for the remainder of the day and evening. What we really needed in this investigation was a break—anything that would move us forward.

It was 1:30 in the afternoon before I got back to the office. I reviewed all the security recordings for the day in search of the briefcase last seen in the lobby of the Mayflower. This took almost three hours with negative results. I felt that it was somehow related to Cohn's private meeting held every other Thursday evening. If they stick to their schedule, there should be another meeting this evening.

I left work at the usual time but instead of heading south on 95, I drove around the city making enough turns and running two red lights to ensure I was not being followed. I parked my car in a lot on 4th Street near Judiciary Square. There is a quiet neighborhood pub in the area where I occasionally grabbed a bite to eat. I was certain Jim had notified WATCH24 of my plan, so I felt somewhat secure. The place seemed crowded for a Thursday evening. Being somewhat of a cynic, I was thinking the way everything is going in the country, there are probably more people drinking after work each day. I found an empty stool at the end of the bar, next to a couple who had no interest in anything but each other. Perfect I thought. The menu was limited, but a club sandwich on rye toast won. I needed to kill a little more than an hour and a half, so I started with a light beer and sipped it for at least thirty minutes before ordering any food. It was about 8:00 p.m. when I started walking back toward the White House. That way my assigned vehicle would not be on the White House grounds and no one would know I was there. The rain had stopped by early in the afternoon and the temperature was so pleasant, I actually enjoyed the walk.

It was not unusual for me to be seen around the White House in the evening. Throughout my career, I had always made a conscious effort to work all shifts. It always helps when your subordinates see the boss, no matter what shift they are working. I made my rounds, talking to all the Secret Service and other employees. As expected, all the agents wanted to know if there was anything new on the investigation of Steve's death. I deliberately stayed out of the West Wing of the White House and went to my office. Polk's office was locked and I could tell there was no one there unless they were sitting in the dark. At exactly 9:45 p.m., I headed to the West Wing. I spoke to several more agents and the cleaning staff. No one else was there. Cohn's office was open, and a member of the cleaning staff was vacuuming the carpet. Why no Thursday evening meeting? Was it being held in another location? Perhaps they thought it was getting "too hot" to meet. I wasn't about to call it a night. I returned to my office and decided I would check the West Wing every half hour.

My cell rang at 10:14 p.m. "The meeting has been moved. Meet me at the corner of Pennsylvania Avenue and 15th Street in 15 minutes," Jim ordered, somewhat excited about the information.

That was an easy walk from the White House and I was there in a little over ten minutes. Within minutes, Jim joined me. "According to the WATCH24 surveillance team, Cohn, Polk, Martino and another Hispanic male are having a dinner meeting right now at the Old Ebbitt Grill," Jim began. "They are seated in a booth in the Corner Bar Room. We are about to join them; just follow my lead."

And there we were, walking up 15th Street and into the Grill like we knew what we were doing. I certainly hoped Jim did, for I had no idea what the plan was. Jim asked for a booth in the Corner Bar Room. The hostess led us into the room and pointed to a booth right near the doorway we just entered. Jim saw where Polk was sitting and noting the booth next to them was empty, stated, "We will take the booth over there." The hostess protested saying that was reserved, but Jim ignored her and rapidly sat in the booth facing Polk. I sat on the other side, my back to the four of them. Somehow I think they were too busy to notice us, or they were just hoping we did not notice them.

"Show time," Jim said with a smile. Suddenly he stood up and very loudly said, "Jeff Polk, I thought that was you over there!" And with that, he stood up, motioned for me to follow and walked over to Jeff. Holding his hand out to shake Jeff's, Jim began. "Twice in one week, quite a coincidence. How are you Jeff?"

Polk reluctantly shook his hand. Jim continued, not giving anyone a chance to say a word. He turned his body facing Cohn, stuck out his hand again and loudly said, "Hi, I'm Jim Bruce." Cohn did not know what to do. He looked like a deer in a spotlight.

Finally, he extended his hand and meekly stated, "Stewart Cohn."

"I know the name," said Jim in the same loud voice, "you are the Chief of Staff to the President. You know, I never met President Sanchez, so Stew, if you don't mind, I am going to call you next week so you can introduce us."

And again, before anyone could say a word, he started shaking Martino's hand and in an even louder voice stated, "You look familiar, but I can't put a name to your face."

In a barely audible voice, Martino replied, "James Martino."

"Oh yeah," Jim said never missing a beat, "your picture was on a wanted poster hanging in my office for years. Boy, you have certainly done well for yourself, for a felon." All the faces at the table were now pale and the expressions were something I had never seen before. Too bad I did not have a camera to capture the moment.

The fourth subject was the unidentified Hispanic male that was with Polk in the Mayflower and both Jim and I knew it. He stuck out his hand toward Jim and in a low voice said, "Orlando Ortega." I was fairly confident that this was the same Hispanic male I saw in the car on 14th Street.

Shaking his hand and without lowering his voice, Jim replied, "I'm sorry, I am a little hard of hearing. Did you say your name was Orlando Ortega?" Ortega nodded his head and Jim continued on. "Well it sure was nice meeting all of you and Jeff, don't forget, we are going to have lunch at the Mayflower some day. Maybe next week I will give you a call."

We returned to our booth, and to be honest, I had a difficult time not laughing out loud. Jim winked and put his finger to his lip indicating that now was not the time to discuss what had just happened or what we saw. I am certain Jim saw it too. The Mayflower briefcase was sitting in the booth between Cohn and Martino. It was immediately obvious to both of us that "all the President's men" had just made a huge error. Certainly, the stakes were going to be dramatically raised.

Jim and I each ordered a sandwich and a drink, not that I was hungry. This time I had a diet soda. With Jim, one never knew what was next on the agenda and I did not want alcohol interfering with my thought process. There was not much talk coming from the next booth. Jim, speaking loud enough to be heard, was talking about all the golf courses he had played. I am not sure he was telling the truth, but that really did not matter. I knew exactly what he was doing. Sitting there in our separate booths reminded me of a "Mexican standoff," no pun intended. Who was going to leave first? Jim answered that question by calling for the check. Jim put $30 on the table and stated, "Shall we go?"

We stood up and Jim again walked over to the four of them and again with a loud voice said, "It was sure nice meeting all of you and I hope you have a pleasant weekend. Hope to see you again." I was behind Jim and when Ortega looked at me, I pretended to take two shots at him just as he had done on 14th Street. He quickly looked away, but I made my point. I was not and would not be intimidated by his threats.

As we were walking out the door, Jim said, "My car is around the corner. I will give you a ride to yours."

Once we got inside Jim's car, Jim and I both laughed like hell. I began, "That was some show you put on in there and before you ask, yes, I also saw the briefcase."

"That was a major screw up on their part and they know it," Jim said in a much more serious tone. "I am sure that you are going to have a tough day tomorrow. Can you handle it?"

"I expect that they will try to transfer me out of the White House tomorrow," I replied, "and I already know how I am going to respond to that."

"Good." Jim continued, "WATCH24 will pick up the surveillance on all four of them when they leave the Grill. We need to determine if Orlando Ortega is really who he says he is and where the briefcase ends up. I will get on that as soon as I drop you off. Where did you park?"

Before I got out of Jim's car, I asked him to again thank his wife for spending some time with Kim the other night. "You know, with our law enforcement careers, they can't help but experience some of the stresses inherent with our jobs," I said purposely.

"I know," Jim said in response. "Thank God we both have understanding wives. Talk to you in the morning."

It was obvious that Jim did not want the conversation to go any further. But I got the sense that Patricia may have told him of her plans.

FRIDAY, AUGUST 31

Again, my trip to work this morning was a blur, which unfortunately is becoming the norm. I have no idea what the day will bring, but given what happened last evening, I knew it was not going to be a routine day by any stretch of the imagination. If ASAC Polk had nothing to hide, he certainly would be in my office first thing this morning. But then again, I knew he did not want to see me today, and likewise, I did not want to see him. I was also sure that I would see President Sanchez today and I just hope I could professionally handle the meeting with some dignity.

I wasn't in my office five minutes when Jim called. "I have some interesting events that you need to know about," Jim began. "The briefcase ended up in Cohn's townhouse. If he doesn't take it to work this morning, we will get a search warrant and remove it once he leaves. Orlando Ortega is not who he says he is, but we still do not have confirmation on a name. We believe he is Orlando Del Toro, one of the main players in the Mexican drug cartels. Everything OK with you Chuck?"

"I am a little nervous about today, but that is to be expected," I responded. "But I will tell you one thing," I continued, "I am ready for whatever happens."

"Good," said Jim. "See you at noon."

The Friday before a three-day Labor Day weekend is almost always slow. We usually have minimum staffing at the White House and quite honestly, not a lot of work is completed. I looked around my office for any indication that anyone had been there since I left last night. Everything seemed to be as I left it. Then the thought came to my mind. Could this be my last day in the

White House? Quite honestly, that was my expectation. I was determined to leave with dignity, so I had some work to do.

I began by going through my desk, removing anything personal and shredding those files which were sensitive. I really did not worry about any type of transition with my replacement since in all likelihood the President would insist on Polk as the new Special Agent-in-Charge. And I would bet that the first task on his list is a sweep for any listening devices.

My goal was to leave the office somewhat sterile, just as I found it a little less than two months ago. That should not be difficult since I never really had the time to hang much on the walls or personalize the office. The truth is that once Polk came aboard, I saw the writing on the wall, and figured my days in the White House were numbered. I never felt fully comfortable in this office, and, in many ways, I was happy to leave it. The bulk of the morning was spent packing a single box to take with me at the end of the day. With the packing and the shredding done, I spent the remainder of the morning composing a single letter to all the Secret Service agents and employees in the White House. I wanted them to know that my departure was not of my choice and how much I appreciated their hard work, dedication and professionalism over the years I was assigned to the White House.

I really had expected to be called into the President's office by noon, but since I had not heard a word, I headed to my car, box in hand. I drove to the Mayflower for our meeting and despite my best efforts, I was again the last to arrive. As I walked through the door, I was pleased to see FBI Deputy Director Tom Wilson was present, increasing our group to seven.

Once we were all seated in a private room with our lunches, I asked that we all take a moment for grace and to remember Steve Oates. After the prayer, Jim began by reviewing the events of the week, emphasizing to Steve Mason that he needed to make notes on any possible charges that could be brought against any of the President's staff. There were a few chuckles when Jim repeated last night's encounter at the Old Ebbitt Grill. But most importantly, Jim outlined the significance of the briefcase that Cohn took to his townhouse last night.

"They made a huge mistake," Jim said. "With the help of Tom, we obtained a search warrant for Cohn's residence and executed it this morning. The briefcase contained $2 million in cash and we now have an official criminal investigation. My guess is that greed is a verb in the Sanchez White House."

That statement from Jim created a lot of chatter among the group. I was the first to speak out loud. "Eight months in office and the President is already getting ready for the next election. Most everyone agrees, he never left the campaign mode."

"You are probably right Chuck, but most important, is the source of the money," added Tom Wilson. "Let me explain my theory," he continued. "We have now positively identified the Latino male with Cohn and company last night as Orlando Del Toro. He is well known by law enforcement in El Paso as the front man for the Mexican drug cartels and although he is not wanted in the States at this time, he is suspected of at least five homicides in Mexico, to include two policemen. We believe that the two million dollars is payment, or perhaps partial payment, to the President for his decreasing the law enforcement resources on the Mexican border and stopping the major Latino gang investigation by the US Attorney in El Paso. Needless to say, those acts make it much easier for the Mexican drug cartels to successfully move drugs and humans across our border.

"We have no idea how Cohn will react when he returns home this evening and finds his two million dollars missing," Jim added. "Our hope is that he immediately thinks Del Toro is responsible, but after last night, he would have to at least consider that we are responsible. We have his phones tapped, so we will know who he calls in his state of panic. There is no doubt that they will now be desperate and will do anything to protect the President. I would expect that Chuck will be removed from the White House, probably by the end of the day. But it will not stop there."

"We now have FBI agents working with WATCH24 personnel on the surveillance of the four targets and on the protection of each of you and your families," Tom added reassuringly.

"I expect that I will be called to the President's Office sometime this afternoon. I am ready and we will see what happens," I told the group. "I will keep Jim up-to-date and I am sure he will let you know."

Steve, who had been quiet until now, spoke up. "In the meantime, I will start drawing up charges from what I have so far. But if anyone has any additional information that you think would be helpful, please call me."

"I like and agree with Tom's theory on the reason for the payment," said General Monroe. "I will work all the intelligence sources this weekend to see if I can add some credible evidence that we can use in court."

Judge Walters turned toward Joe Wells and stated, "Joe, I have a question for you. Did your wife get that presidential appointment yet?"

"She had her final interview yesterday and I expect she will hear something early next week. Why do you ask?" Joe replied.

"If they do a background, how is she going to respond when she is asked what you do?" the Judge asked.

"I imagine she will say I am retired, Judge. What are you inferring?" Joe responded apparently somewhat defensively. He continued, "She knows nothing about this group or what we are doing."

"You are missing my point, Joe," Judge Walters said calmly, "You are an extremely valuable part of this team and I just want to make sure that nothing we do interferes with your wife getting the position she wants or brings any stress to your marriage. But if our lives are in danger, and obviously they are, how do you explain all of this to your wife?"

"I already have taken care of that," Joe said. "I told her that given my work over the years, we always need to take certain precautions to remain safe. She never asks any questions."

"That's a good point for all of us," Jim quickly added, trying to end the exchange between Joe and Judge Walters. All of us recognized that Joe thought his loyalty was in question, which couldn't be further from the truth.

Jim continued, "We all want our families to be safe, but we need not give them all the details of what our team is doing. Use your best judgment knowing this is a top secret assignment."

We all talked for another half hour and outlined what we needed to do to move forward. Jim ended the meeting by stating, "We have no idea what lies ahead, but I believe we now have the upper hand. That in itself makes the enemy more dangerous. I would expect that within the next week, we will see a lot of activity. We can only hope and pray that they make another major error. Each of you be careful and remember, we believe they have already committed one murder to protect their agenda. May our Constitution remain our guiding document and with the good Lord's support, may we remain strong in protecting it from the enemies within."

Once we got up from the table, Joe immediately went to speak to the Judge. From the conversation at the meeting, I again had the feeling that Judge Walters didn't trust Joe's wife not to tell all. Joe and Jackie have only been married for a little over a year. It is the second marriage for both. Jim had mentioned to me earlier that Jackie's oldest son was arrested by the Drug Enforcement Agency and is currently serving time in federal prison. I am sure that Judge Walters knows that as well. I trust Joe and we cannot afford to lose him from our team. He is doing the right thing by not confiding in his wife. The rest of us left the room, leaving the two of them to reconcile their differences.

It was 1:40 p.m. before I got back to the office and still no messages. I really expected to be summoned to the President's Oval Office by now. I spent the next hour deleting as much as I could from my computer. I knew they could recover it if they were so inclined, but I had always been cautious when sending emails and composing letters on my computer. In any case, it made me feel better. I also changed all my passwords to access Secret Service files and eliminated my address book, for what reason I do not know.

The phone rang at exactly three o'clock. The message was simple. "The President wants you in the Oval Office immediately!" There is no chance one could misinterpret that message. Normally, I would immediately rush down the hallway in order to keep the President from waiting. Not this time. I sat back to collect my thoughts for ten minutes and then leisurely walked to the Oval Office.

The door was ajar, and I could see Stewart Cohn sitting there as well. I knocked and Cohn stated, "Come in."

"Yes sir, Mr. President," I said with authority. No one asked me to sit, so I stood there waiting for some sort of response.

The President spoke first, "Burke, what in the hell are you doing?"

I was ready. "My job, sir," is how I answered.

"Really," the President stated. "Well, I do not believe that you are an appropriate fit for my administration, so you will be reassigned effective close of business today. You are to report to Secret Service Headquarters next Tuesday morning."

"I would rather stay in my current assignment until I retire, Mr. President," I said throwing him slightly off guard.

"That's not possible," the President said sternly.

"Yes sir," I said not backing down, "You do what you have to do sir, and I will do what I have to do."

Cohn spoke up, "What does that mean, Burke?"

I was quick to say, "I think you know exactly what that means, Mr. Cohn."

I could see that the President did not like the way this conversation was going and said, "That's it, Mr. Burke."

"Yes sir," I said as I headed toward the door, pausing to add, "And exactly what are you doing, Mr. President?" I closed the door behind me, not waiting for a response. I walked down the hall with my dignity intact, thinking if I could only hear the conversation now taking place in the Oval Office.

I returned to my office and made sure I had taken everything that was personal or needed. I then sat down at my computer and sent my letter to one group, "Secret Service all," knowing every White House Secret Service employee would read it by Tuesday morning. Before sending it, I excluded ASAC Jeff Polk from the recipients. By the time he heard about it, it would be too late for him to stop it from being distributed. I kept my White House pass from the past administration for sentimental reasons, knowing Polk would invalidate it on the computer as soon as I walked out the door. What he did not know however, is that I have a card that would bypass the security system that was to be used in extreme emergencies only. You never knew when one could have an "extreme emergency."

"Not only life, but living with others is possible because of law. Without law, no man could be assured of the fruits of his labors. Without law, brute force would prevail, the weak would be destroyed by the strong and the strong would destroy themselves in their struggles for ascendancy. Without law there would be no peace or privacy, no protection of persons or property, public or private; no foreseeable future, no assurance of anything we could count on."
—Aristotle 321 BC

CHAPTER 10

MONDAY, SEPTEMBER 3

The kids came home for the weekend, and I could not begin to tell you how much that meant to both Kim and me. We had spent the last two days as a family with dinner at a rather expensive restaurant on Saturday night and a cookout on Sunday after church. Last night, we had a serious discussion on what was happening to our country and at Kim's insistence, we talked about how we have provided for each of them should something happen to us. It was a sobering conversation for everyone. We ended the night with a board game and some snacks, in an effort to hold on to some normalcy in the midst of this madness.

After a hardy breakfast this morning, we sent Tom and Marie back to college with some extra cash and a bag of home baked cookies. They appeared happy and again seemed to take all of this in stride. Good for them. I did not want my actions to change their lives in any way. To put things in their proper prospective, I thought about the fact that there is no more rewarding accomplishment in life than seeing your children as intelligent, self assured, happy adults.

Kim and I had a relaxing afternoon again spending time planning our retirement. I knew with my seniority, the Secret Service could not transfer me out of the Metro Washington area. My best guess is that I would have an administrative position in Headquarters until I retire. If there were no openings, they would probably create a temporary position doing some unnecessary task. It did not matter to me as long as I had some flexibility to fulfill my obligations to the group—"The DC Seven" as Kim so fondly named us. Little did I know the name would stick.

All in all, it was a normal three-day holiday weekend in spite of this past week's events. What I found strange was that I felt relaxed, probably because I truly believed we had the upper hand. After all, we are on the right side and the good guys almost always win.

TUESDAY, SEPTEMBER 4

When the phone rings in the middle of the night it's never good news. It was 4:30 a.m. and my cell phone was ringing. I heard Kim say, "Oh no, not again." I had been in a deep sleep, but managed to get it on the fifth ring.

"Chuck," the familiar voice said, "this is Jim, good morning." I was able to mumble something, and Jim continued. "Everything is OK, but I am at your back door. You and your wife need to come downstairs and let me in. But listen, do not turn on any lights, understand?"

That got my attention. "We will be right there," I said in a low voice. I told Kim what Jim had said, but even with only the night light, I could see the look of apprehension on her face. We quietly moved downstairs in the darkness and I opened the door and let Jim and another man into the kitchen.

"Can we all sit at the kitchen table?" Jim asked. I motioned and we all sat down.

The lights from the digital clocks on the appliances gave us enough light to at least see each other. "Kim, Chuck, this is Ben from WATCH24; he is about to become one of your best friends." Kim and I looked at each other with puzzled faces. "Let me explain," Jim continued. "Ben called me about 1:00 a.m. this morning to report the movement of two men around your home. They were not here to harm you at that time, but here to place explosives in your car, Chuck, so you would be killed when you started the car this morning."

Kim put her hand to her mouth, and I could see the tears flowing.

Jim went on, "I had to make a quick decision and told Ben to let them complete their task and I would have an FBI surveillance team follow them as soon as they completed their dirty deed. They left here and had breakfast in an all-night diner just off Interstate 95. After eating they drove to Dulles Airport and are just now returning their rental car. I imagine they will be boarding a plane shortly and we will be on them until we figure out what is going on. In the meantime, we are getting arrest warrants for both of them—John Doe and Jim Doe for now, until we know their names. But now we have some decisions to make. Chuck, what if we let the car explode by remote start and let them think you are dead? Kim, you would immediately call 911 and then call me on my home phone, but I would actually be close by. I would have the FBI do the investigation and no one would know you were not in the vehicle. Kim, I will take you away from this horrible scene. I will send someone to pick up Tom and Marie, not telling them anything. And the four of you will be discussing the entire incident at a remote vacation home near Charlottesville where you can be safe until this is over. Ben and Carol, another WATCH24 agent will be with you around the clock. And Chuck, you will still be involved in the investigation, and we will figure out when it is best for you to reappear. I am hoping that the blast will generate a call to Polk or Cohn and we will have it recorded. That would mean that someone from their group would have to be in the area to report it and that is why I did not want you to use any lights." Suddenly there was a woman standing next to the table; I never heard her or saw her come in. Ben introduced Carol to each of us.

"The downside of all of this," Jim explained, "is that the bomb is going to explode. We took a quick look and the blast will probably do some damage to your home and there will be a fire. Kim, you will be upstairs with Carol. The blast will not harm you as long as you stay in the rear of the house. Neither one of your neighbors' homes is in the blast zone, but there may be some broken glass. We can call the bomb squad, but we can't guarantee the bomb will not explode and unfortunately Cohn and company will definitely know we have protection teams on all of you. That will make our job much more difficult. Chuck, I realize by putting it this way, I haven't given you much of a choice, but there is a lot at risk here. It's your call."

I sat there holding Kim's hand. Through her tears she laughed and asked if our homeowner's insurance was up to date. I nodded and immediately knew how to answer Jim's question. "What do we do next?" I asked.

Jim gave us his usual smile. "Pretend we were never here and go back to bed. Get up at your normal time and get dressed for work. Each of you pack a suitcase and leave it under the bed. Ben and Carol will be sitting right here to guide you the rest of the way."

Needless to say, sleep was out of the question for two reasons. Who could sleep after that conversation? And we normally get up at 5:30 a.m. and it was now 5:05. We held each other hoping that in a few short hours our family would be safe and together again.

We went through our normal morning routine which was anything but normal. We could smell the coffee and bacon from downstairs so we knew breakfast would not be a problem. We went down together and sat at the table with Ben and Carol. We ate eggs and bacon while they briefed us. I was to walk out the front door as I usually do and then quickly go to the garage side of the house where Ben would lead me to a vehicle one street over, waiting for us. Once we heard the explosion, we would drive away before all the emergency equipment arrived. Kim was to stay in the rear bathroom with her cell phone until the explosion. Her first call would be to 911 and her second call to Jim's home phone. She was to go out the back door and wait in the backyard until Carol, acting as a neighbor, came to comfort her. As we were finalizing our plan, the suitcases were brought downstairs by a

WATCH24 agent and taken out the back door. With about ten minutes remaining before I left for work, my nerves were raw. On the outside Kim looked relatively calm; however, I was certain she was nervous as well. When the time came, I hugged her more than most days, kissed her and whispered, "Everything will be OK."

She whispered back, "I know. Let's trust the Lord." With that, Kim went upstairs and I went out the front door.

The plan went down without a hitch and as soon as we got to the car, I heard and felt the explosion. It was much greater than I anticipated, and I immediately was concerned for Kim. Ben's phone rang instantly, and he answered in literally a second. "Kim's fine," he reported and our car left the curb. Just as we were leaving the neighborhood, the first police car went by us heading for the house. Once on the main road, we could see and hear a fire truck and ambulance heading toward the neighborhood. Then it came to me how absolutely insane this President really is.

I could tell that Ben took all the right precautions to ensure our safety. Obviously, with my Secret Service experience, I knew a little about protecting individuals. I went over my checklist which had been embedded in my brain for years just to see if Ben had missed anything. He hadn't. I finally spoke. "You must have some Secret Service experience. I have been watching you and you have taken every possible precaution to keep me safe."

"No sir," Ben responded, "I am a retired Navy Seal. But I did attend the weeklong Secret Service school about ten years ago."

"It is obvious to me that you must have paid attention in class."

"I did and I did gain some experience in VIP security when I was assigned to the Pentagon for a little over a year."

"How did you end up with WATCH24?" I asked.

"A friend of mine told me he was going to apply for a position with a relatively new top notch security company and thought I should apply also. My wife was anxious for me to get out of the Navy and I had my time in, so I applied for a position with WATCH24. They made me an offer I could not refuse. I retired from the Navy and here I am.

We traveled on so many back roads in northern Virginia that I had no idea what county we were in, nor did I recognize any landmarks. After exactly one hour and 50 minutes, I know because I timed it, we pulled down a long gravel driveway to what appeared to be a fairly new small ranch home. We were greeted at the door by a young, petite, rather attractive woman who introduced herself as Sharon, a WATCH24 agent. Sharon explained that she had been assigned to protect Marie at college and had actually befriended her pretending to be another William and Mary student. Jim sent her here knowing that with all that has happened, Marie may need some extra support. I can't tell you the comfort I felt knowing Marie was so well protected, but even more comforting was how professional and thorough this WATCH24 organization was handling this crazy assignment they were given. Knowing Jim, I guess I would expect no less.

The house had an eat in kitchen, a very large great room, three bedrooms and two baths. The attached two car garage was already being taken over by WATCH24. Three cots and apparently some electronic equipment were sitting on the floor. As I was taking a quick tour, I noticed our suitcases on the bed in the master bedroom. I could not help but wonder how long this was going to be "home" for the four of us.

Ben sat down with me and reviewed the security procedures that would keep all of us safe. There was no doubt in my mind that we could be a bit more relaxed here than we had been for the last several days. The kids will be fine, but I am a little concerned about Kim.

All of this is a lot to digest in such a short period of time. There is no telling how hearing the explosion and seeing the damage to the house would affect her. I guess this is a necessary step if we are ever going to have a successful conclusion to this horrific episode. It troubles me that my family has to suffer through this, which in turn tells me much about the mindset of the enemy within.

Tom was the first to arrive. I met him in the driveway. We were both relieved to see each other and we hugged longer and harder than usual. "What's going on Dad?" Tom asked with great concern in his voice.

"Everyone is all right, Son. Mom and Marie will be here shortly; then we will sit down and I will explain everything. In the meantime, your bedroom is at the end of the hallway so go ahead and put your suitcase in your room." I watched as Tom walked to the house. Sharon opened the door and introduced herself by name only. I couldn't help but notice the instant smile on Tom's face and again I thought how brilliant Jim really is.

Tom and I were outside when Marie arrived about a half hour later. She had the same question as her brother and I gave the same response. When Marie saw Sharon, they hugged and laughed together, confusing Tom more than ever. And finally, after what seemed like an eternity, Kim and Carol pulled into the driveway. The family reunion lasted a good ten minutes. We all went inside and there on the table was a pot of coffee, orange juice and a plate of pastry. Ben, Carol and Sharon headed for the garage so that we could have our privacy. I was about to destroy the naive world of my children, just as I had destroyed Kim's a week ago.

"One great, strong unselfish soul in every community could

actually redeem the world."
—Elbert Hubbard

CHAPTER 11

As soon as we sat at the table, I could see that Tom and Marie wanted answers and that any other conversation would be superficial. I started from the beginning leaving out only the very minor details. If I missed anything important, Kim quickly corrected me. I could see the part about Steve's murder visibly upset them and Kim's tears did not help. I paused just before I started explaining what happened this morning and noted that both my children were wide eyed and somewhat in shock from what they already heard. Neither had even sipped their coffee, let alone touched a pastry.

I carefully explained the call from Jim this morning and the plan. "So for all intent and purpose, I was killed in the explosion," I said with a slight smile. Wrong choice of words; there were tears everywhere even a few running down Tom's cheeks. "Hold on," I added, "no one was hurt in the explosion. However, I am not certain about the damage to the house; I didn't see it, but your mother did."

Kim jumped right in, "The front of the house and the garage are pretty much destroyed. I am not sure about my car inside the garage, but most of our furniture and personal property appears to have been spared."

I picked up the conversation again. "I cannot tell you how long we will have to stay here, but for now you will not be able to contact any of your friends. In case you don't know it, I will tell you that your cell phones have been stripped of their batteries so no one could track us here. We do have a regular phone here, but do not use it or answer it, unless you talk to me first. We will be safe here and WATCH24 personnel will be with us all the time. There will be an announcement that there will be a private memorial service for me, so that will bring closure to my death and there will be no need to attend any pretend service. So sit tight and I will get you back to school as soon as I know it is safe. Any questions?"

Tom was the first to speak, "One question. Is Sharon single?"

With that, Marie poked him in his side and we all had a much needed laugh, which actually released some of the tension in the room. Marie followed with, "On a more serious note Dad, will you keep us up-to-date on what is going on?"

"I promise," I answered.

With that, Marie turned to Tom and stated, "Yes, she is single," and we had another giggle.

We watched the local news channels and the cable news channels for the coverage of the bombing. The pictures of the house again brought out the tears in Kim and Marie. Actually, I was quite surprised there was not more destruction. The garage had the most damage from the fire and it was obvious to me that Kim was going to need a new car. FBI Deputy Director Tom Wilson was the official spokesman for the investigation and would only say that a senior federal law enforcement official was killed in the explosion and it will take several days to positively identify the body. The local reporter stated that they have confirmed that this was the home of Charles Burke, who was the Special Agent-in-Charge of the Secret Service at the White House, but they could not confirm that he was the one killed in the explosion this morning. As expected, a White House spokesman stated they had no comment at this time. It will be interesting to hear their comment once the identity is confirmed.

It was 4:00 p.m. before I heard from Jim or anyone else for that matter. "Did you see the coverage on the television?" Jim asked.

"We watched it for a while, but it appears there will be no additional information released for several days," I said jokingly.

"And as you know, that is by design," Jim added. "Tom told the White House that the body was in so many pieces that the lab would have to do a multiple DNA analysis before they would confirm it's you. That gives us time to plan our next moves. Martino got the first call this morning from a cell with a Texas area code. The male's only word was 'bang' and the phone went dead. Martino then called Cohn and stated, 'First assignment completed' and he hung up the phone. Unfortunately, Cohn did not call the President, so we have not tied him to this yet."

"What about the two who placed the bomb?"

"They flew to El Paso and are currently under surveillance by the FBI. They will be quietly arrested before the end of the day. The rental car has been seized and taken to the FBI lab," Jim answered.

"And what did Martino mean by first assignment?" I continued.

"The problem," Jim explained, "is that we know there are more assignments, but we don't know how many. I would imagine I am the target of assignment number two and we have taken some extra precautions. Since we do not know if there are any additional assignments, Tom has increased the protection on all members of our group."

"What about your family?" I continued with my questions.

"WATCH24 has everyone covered. Is everybody doing OK there?"

"Everyone is fine and both my son and daughter thank you for sending Sharon," I stated.

"First assignment completed," Jim said laughing. We spoke for another minute and Jim ended by promising he would be back in touch at about 9:00 this evening.

It has been less than 12 hours since this entire bomb episode started and only a little more than seven hours that I have been sequestered to this house. Yet, I so much wanted to be back as part of our group. I wonder how much longer I will have to stay here before the walls start closing in. On the other hand, perhaps I should be counting my blessings. My family is here and I would not want to do anything to jeopardize their safety. I guess I just do not enjoy being dead.

WATCH24 personnel were doing an outstanding job taking care of us. Tom and Marie seemed quite comfortable here; Kim seemed to be more relaxed as the afternoon passed. Carol brought out several board games, two decks of cards and several of the most recent magazines to help us prevent the boredom that would eventually overtake us.

Kim decided she wanted to do all the cooking to stay busy and immediately recruited Marie as her assistant. Carol agreed to do all the grocery shopping as long as she had a list. Kim suggested that we all eat together, however, Ben said only one WATCH24 member would be free to eat at a time, so they would have to rotate. Given the circumstances, it could be no better.

Dinner consisted of London broil, baked potatoes and a tossed salad. I was not surprised to see that Sharon was the first to join us for a meal. Kim and I were pretty much left out of the conversation, but we actually enjoyed listening to an innocent, light hearted conversation, which we had not heard in quite some time. After dinner, we moved to the great room for coffee and dessert so we could watch the news. Nothing had changed from the earlier news shows with one exception. The local news was stating that they had from a reliable source that the deceased was Charles Burke, a high ranking member of the Secret Service assigned to the White House. My best bet was that Jeff Polk was that source.

Jim called at 9:00 p.m. as promised. What I did not expect was that I would be attending a meeting of our full group by speaker phone. I excused myself from everyone and went to the master bedroom where I could have some privacy.

Jim started with an announcement, "And from Heaven above, we are pleased to have Chuck with us this evening. How are you Chuck?" I couldn't help my response, "Alive and well and how are all of you?" which drew immediate laughter from all.

The levity did not last long. Jim got right down to business. "On a serious note, we are fortunate to have Chuck with us tonight and I want to give the credit to WATCH24 personnel who are doing an outstanding job keeping all of us safe." With that everyone applauded. Jim continued, "Needless to say, Cohn and company by their actions have moved this investigation to the highest notch, meaning that we need to do the same. We do not have time on our side any longer; we need to move rapidly and convene a grand jury as soon as possible. Let me explain the situation. With a lot of additional resources from Tom, the FBI arrested both the Hispanic males who planted the bomb in Chuck's car just before they crossed the border back into Mexico. They have refused to talk and have asked for an attorney. An El Paso judge, who is definitely on our side, will allow us to keep them in seclusion, without any calls so we can move forward with our investigation. More importantly, we know that there are additional assignments planned and we believe that I am one of their targets, but that is all we know. Obviously, we cannot risk any additional loss of life so again we have to move rapidly. The major problem, as I see it, is that we have only very minimal circumstantial evidence tying the President to any criminal act, unless someone rolls. So Judge, how long before we can convene a grand jury?"

"I believe we can have one by Friday," the Judge stated, "and there is no reason we should not hold them through the weekend."

"And Steve," Jim went on, "can you be ready to present evidence on Friday?"

"I am going to need another attorney to get ready and present a solid case," Steve responded.

Tom spoke up immediately, "I will have a good one for you in the morning."

Jim again spoke, "Now the rest of us need to get our ducks in a row to ensure we have enough evidence. Any thoughts?"

Joe Wells was the first to speak. "It would help if we could do something overtly that causes panic in the White House which in turn generates some unplanned phone calls. These types of calls almost always give us additional information."

I jumped right in at that point. "What would you think if tomorrow night after everyone leaves the White House, say about 10:30 p.m., Tom calls Polk to tell him that the deceased man in the bombing is not Charles Burke and he wanted to tell him before he heard it on the eleven o'clock news? He could add that the problem is that no one knows where I am. We then should be able to follow the chain of phone calls beginning with Polk to Cohn and see how far it goes." There was silence in the group.

"I think that is a great idea," said Jim.

"Works for me!" added Joe.

"Cohn and his cronies will all be looking over their shoulders," Tom concluded.

General Monroe was next to speak, "Let me fill you in on some recent intelligence. According to a very reliable source, President Sanchez has convened a panel of trusted friends to explore the feasibility of amending the United States Constitution to allow him unlimited terms as President of the United States. He realizes that this will take him more than one term to accomplish, so the first step is to win reelection. Even though this is his first year in office, he and Cohn have a comprehensive plan that they feel will ensure his re-election. A major part of that plan is to obtain as much money as possible which will be distributed and eventually flow back to him as campaign donations. That, I believe, was the purpose of the $2 million and I find it hard to believe that was the first briefcase filled with money that went to the White House. Think back about our discussion on the President's border policy and you pretty much have an outline of President Sanchez's agenda. He must be stopped and the sooner, the better."

The meeting lasted another 20 minutes. Unless something dramatic happened, we had a plan. Joe promised to call each of us after midnight on Thursday to update us on any information from the phone calls we hoped to generate. My hope and prayer was that the end of the Sanchez Administration was in sight.

As I walked back in the great room, each one turned toward me and waited. Finally Tom spoke, "So what's new?"

"Suffice it to say, that I will be returning from the dead; however, I am now a missing person. More on the 11:00 o'clock news tomorrow evening." That did not satisfy anyone.

Marie turned off the television and ordered, "OK Dad, let's hear the full story." I sat down and started from the beginning. They deserved to know the truth.

WEDNESDAY, SEPTEMBER 5

I heard the phone ring only once and looked at the clock—1:22 a.m. My heart skipped a beat. There was a knock on the master bedroom door and Ben opened the door slightly. "Mr. Burke, you need to pick up the phone," he said softly. Both Kim and I sat up immediately and I grabbed the phone.

"Are you awake?" Tom Wilson asked.

"I am now and if you are calling at this hour," I said, "I am not sure I want to hear what you are about to tell me."

"The second assignment just took place," Tom said in a serious voice. "Two men tried to break into Jim's house, probably to assassinate him. When confronted by WATCH24 and FBI agents, a gun fight ensued. Unfortunately, Jim's wife was shot and is in critical condition. Jim is with her at the hospital right now. One of the bad guys is dead, the other escaped, but they have set up a perimeter and hopefully they will get him as well. I wish I had better news, but I will keep you up-to-date."

"Tom, what can I do? I feel so helpless here in this hide-away."

"For now, just sit tight and keep Patricia and Jim in your prayers. I am heading up the investigation. I think we should let this one take its natural course and have the FBI do a full press release without giving up any sensitive information. What do you think?"

"I would like to know if the wires picked up any pertinent phone calls first," I responded.

"You make a good point. I will check and get back to you in a couple of hours," Tom concluded.

By the time I hung up the phone, Kim was frantic. I told her what I knew. She cried uncontrollably and began shaking. "What is this world coming to?" she asked. "If Patricia had left to live with their daughter, this would not have happened."

There is little I could say to ease the pain Kim was feeling. I tried convincing her that we needed to get some more rest, for tomorrow was going to be another busy day. But needless to say, neither of us could sleep.

It was 3:50 a.m. before Tom called back. "You were right," Tom started, "Martino called Polk at about 2:00 a.m. telling him it did not go well. He told him Hector was shot and Ramon was in his rental car in a parking lot, not knowing what to do. We are still looking for him. I do not believe they know that Patricia was shot at this time. Strange we did not pick up a call to Martino, so he must have a phone we are not covering. Polk seemed a bit panic-stricken."

"Did Polk call Cohn?" I asked.

"Not yet, I think he is scared to call and wake him with the bad news."

"Any news on Patricia's condition?"

"She's in the operating room right now and Jim said he would call you as soon as he can,"

"What is our next step?" I inquired.

"Just like I said earlier, we are letting it go to the press, with one additional piece of information. The press report is going to state that Jim is missing also. With both of you missing, Polk and Cohn will be paranoid and hopefully do something stupid."

"And what are we going to do about Martino?"

"I am not sure yet, but I will call you later today," Tom said as he hung up.

I was up now and Kim had finally fallen back asleep, so I went to the kitchen to make some coffee. Ben was sitting at the table in the dark already having a cup. He turned on a small flashlight and asked me how I wanted my coffee as he got up to get it. "Black," I told him and sat down. Ben already knew what had happened and I updated him on Jim's wife. For the next two hours, Ben and I sat there talking about what was happening to our country and everything else under the sun. Ben was an interesting man— intelligent, college graduate with two degrees, a Navy veteran, and family man. He certainly is the person you want next to you when things get tough. At exactly six o'clock, Ben turned on the kitchen light. He explained that Carol and Sharon use thermal imaging and night vision to make sure the outside perimeter is clear and their job is easier and safer if there are no lights on in the house. If they had any doubt, they would have let him know and the lights would not have been turned on. They certainly have their act together. Carol came into the kitchen and grabbed a cup of coffee and headed back to the garage. Ben explained that she would be watching the perimeter cameras for the next three hours.

Sharon came into the kitchen next and asked what I would like for breakfast. "Why don't we let everyone else sleep and I will eat with the two of you," I said, "and your choice." It was bacon and eggs with home fries and it really tasted good. I knew we could not stay in this house forever, but right now it was quite safe considering the circumstances.

The phone rang again at 6:20 a.m. "Polk called Cohn at six o'clock," Tom said with excitement. "After he filled him in on the events from earlier in the morning, Cohn stated, 'I think the President would like to see Martino disappear. I will get back to you.' And we are going to take care of that. I think we should quietly pick him up as a material witness in protective custody and see if the Judge will allow us to hold him for a few days without him making any calls. With him missing, the White House will be in a panic as well. The missing persons' list keeps growing."

"I like that idea," I said, "and it looks like the number of charges is growing as well."

"Like weeds; I will call you later," Tom stated as he hung up the phone.

We turned on the local news and watched the story of the "apparent attempted murder of another high ranking federal law enforcement official and his family," and the death of one of the suspects. They never even mentioned that Jim was retired or that his wife was in the hospital. Then they went on to state that Jim was missing and speculated that this was related to "yesterday's bombing of another high-ranking federal law enforcement official." The story ended with the news anchor saying, "There are a lot of questions surrounding these two cases, but so far, very few answers." Perfect, I thought. My best guess is that the Oval Office will be busy this morning.

The latest phone call woke Kim, and she came out of the bedroom just in time to watch the news. After the news, I went to the kitchen, got her a cup of coffee and when I handed it to her, I noticed that Ben and Sharon had quietly left the room. I took this opportunity to bring Kim up-to-date on all that happened this morning.

"When is this whole mess going to be over, so we can return to a normal life?" she asked wearily.

"Within a week," I promised, knowing that we would never be able to return to the life we once had a short time ago.

Jim finally called at 9:00 a.m. He told us that Patricia was doing a little better but was still critical. The bullet pierced her lung and damaged her spinal cord. The FBI was arranging to fly their daughter to Washington so she could be with her mother. "I am not leaving Patricia's side until our daughter arrives at the hospital, so you are going to have to get along without me for a while," Jim said. "Tom is calling me regularly to keep me updated on the case, but right now, Patricia is my primary concern."

"I fully understand Jim," I said. "I wish there was something that Kim and I could do. But be assured that both of you are in our prayers."

"Thanks, right now that is what we need," Jim said as he ended the call.

Typical college kids, Tom and Marie got up about 10:00 a.m.

and immediately asked "What's for breakfast?" I sat with Kim, Tom and Marie while they ate their eggs and bacon. I brought the kids up-to-date omitting some of the details I had earlier given Kim. They were not as detail driven as their mother, but they did ask about Patricia's condition. They have known Jim and Patricia for a lot of years and were shaken by what had happened during the night. They too wanted to know when this whole mess would end.

The day passed rather slowly and not knowing what was happening minute by minute was driving me up a wall. I did not want to call Jim; he had enough on his mind. My wife could see that I was a bit tense, but said nothing. The kids had settled in and were actually studying in anticipation of going back to college in a few days. Finally, the phone rang at about 4:10 p.m. and I grabbed it quickly. "I know you are probably going stir crazy, so I thought I would bring you up to speed," said Tom. "We did not get Martino alone until about 2:00 this afternoon when he was walking to a late lunch. The Judge says we can hold him for 72 hours, but we can't talk to him without allowing him to make a phone call. We were very nice to him, but he knows it's over, so he has some time to think about it. It will be a while before the White House figures he's missing. Hopefully, that will generate more conversation this evening. The Judge also gave us a search warrant for his apartment, which did not give us any additional information."

"I still think Polk is the one who is going to fold," I told Tom. "In any case, he's our best bet at this time."

"You are probably right," Tom agreed and added, "Why don't you come up with a plan on when and how to approach him. Just keep in mind that we still need to better substantiate that the

President was an active participant in all of this. It would a crying shame if after all we have been through and after all the turmoil they have caused, the President is able to walk away unscathed."

"I will see what I can come up with and rest assured, the President will not be able to wash his hands from all of this," I said as we hung up our phones. For the first time, I believed there could be an actual end to this nightmare we have been living.

"Make us to choose the harder right instead of the easier wrong,

and never to be content with a half truth when the whole can be won. Endow us with courage that is born of loyalty to all that is noble and worthy, that scorns to compromise with vice and injustice and knows no fear when truth and right are in jeopardy."
—From the West Point Cadet Prayer

CHAPTER 12

THURSDAY, SEPTEMBER 6

I finally got a full night's sleep without any phone calls. That generally meant that all went as planned last evening. More than likely, Jim was probably getting phone calls from Tom, but they elected to let me sleep. I got up early to watch the news. It was still the lead story, with nothing new reported. What was interesting was the second story announcing that James Martino, the Hispanic Liaison Czar for the White House had suddenly resigned yesterday. When questioned about his departure, the White House had "no comment at this time."

What happened? Had someone seen the FBI take him off the street yesterday? More likely, was there someone in the FBI feeding the White House? I wonder if Tom knew about this. I quickly dialed his number, but got his voicemail. Out of habit, I dialed Jim's number.

"How's Patricia?" I asked.

"No improvement, so please keep her in your prayers."

"What's going on with the news and Martino? I asked Jim.

"I saw it too, Chuck," Jim quickly stated, "I have no idea what happened. I will call Tom and one of us will call you back shortly."

Talk about a monkey wrench in the operation. I can see it now; they push all of this off on Martino and they walk away, free to continue their agenda. I wonder what the telephone intercepts produced last night. Jim never mentioned anything about that. I can't believe they are smarter than we are. Now I am really climbing the walls. What in the hell went wrong? Ten minutes ago, I thought all this would be over in a week. Right now I feel like we are starting all over again. What a roller coaster ride!

Kim was not happy as I explained all this over breakfast. Likewise, several days ago she had believed the end was in sight. Kim had questions, but I did not have the answers. Unfortunately, we found ourselves in what I would call a holding pattern; but most importantly, for now, we were safe.

By 11:00 a.m. I felt I had to do something productive, so I first called Tom. As he answered the phone, he said, "Sorry, I should have gotten back to you sooner. I think that this had all been prearranged. If things started 'going south,' the President and Cohn would have Martino take the hit. If he kept his mouth shut and did not implicate others, his family would be well provided for until he is paroled. That's what we believe at this moment."

"Makes sense," I said. "So what's the battle plan?"

"We only have until Monday to make something happen. I guess we have to see what the indictments look like before we decide. I called Steve and he is now going over all the evidence and material with Antonio Lopez, who is the FBI attorney that I provided to assist him. He promised to give me a status report late in the day."

"Did you find Ramon, the second gunman?" I asked.

"Not yet," Tom responded, "but we have not given up. There must be 60 or 70 officers checking the I95 corridor from Richmond to Baltimore."

"And the two the FBI picked up in Texas before they crossed the border?" I continued asking.

"They still aren't talking," Tom said with a disappointment in his voice.

"I would bet that one or more of the four are responsible for Steve Oaks murder," I stated.

"You are probably right," Tom concluded.

"Tom, what can I do to help, in addition to coming up with a strategy on Polk's interrogation?" was my final question.

His response was instant. "Keep praying, Chuck, keep praying."

To say I had a long, boring afternoon, or to be most blunt, a lousy afternoon, would be an understatement. I worked on some questions to ask Polk during his interrogation but did not come up with a good strategy to ensure success. He is definitely going to be charged, and in most likelihood, will spend the rest of his life in prison. But what would make him want to cooperate. He is not married, has no children, apparently lacks any moral compass and is not very religious. If he believes that President Sanchez will

give him a pardon, he will "lawyer up" and we will be "washed up."
I switched gears and started to analyze what Martino would do,
remembering he is a convicted felon and has been through all of
this before. Will he be the good soldier and quietly take the fall?
What will he do if he knows the President is going down as well?
How will he feel if he thinks Polk is telling us everything? How
about Cohn? He is divorced, lives alone and has an ego the size
of a football stadium. Does he believe that he and the President
can walk away from all of this, leaving Martino out to dry? How
does he explain the $2 million seized from his townhouse? What
about President Sanchez? There is no doubt in my mind that he
and Cohn masterminded every step in this operation. Yet, we do
not really have anything that ties him to any crime. I suddenly
realized that this saga was not coming to an end and felt sick to my
stomach. We still have a long road ahead of us and here I sit—alive,
but rather helpless. I really wanted to go visit Jim and Patricia in
the hospital, but knew that would not be a wise move at this time.

The six o'clock news was much more interesting than I
imagined. The local news stations were now speculating that
the death of Steve Oates was somehow related to the bombing
and the attempted murder of Jim. I suspect they do not realize
how accurate they are. But most interesting was the report by an
undisclosed White House source that former White House Czar
James Martino was also reported missing. To quote the news
anchor, "There seems to be a growing mystery surrounding the
White House that leaves too many unanswered questions and too
many people unaccounted for. Yet, the White House has had no
comment."

It's about time the main street media started questioning the actions of President Sanchez. Until now, he has been enjoying a "love fest" with most of the media. He has had a free ride and the major networks have not been fulfilling their role as "the fourth leg of our democracy." It will be interesting to see how they react when all the facts are known.

I know this sounds strange, but my spirits were lifted after the evening news. Linking Steve's murder to the White House and reporting Martino missing made me wonder who was really feeding the media. By best guess was that somehow Jim's hand was in all of this.

Tom called at about 9:00 p.m. with an update. Nothing of any significance has occurred. The grand jury would be seated by noon tomorrow and both Tom and Jim wanted me ready to testify by 1:00 p.m. Sharon would drive me to DC tomorrow and after my testimony, I would return to the house. Jim's daughter had arrived at the hospital, so Jim, Tom and I would have an hour or so to discuss our next steps before I actually had to report to the grand jury room. Finally, I had something to look forward to.

FRIDAY, SEPTEMBER 7

Sharon and I had an open, frank discussion on the way to Washington. I asked her how she got involved with WATCH24. She explained that she had graduated from college three years ago at age 21 with a degree in criminal justice and was commissioned a Second Lieutenant in the United States Army through the Reserve Officers Training Corp (ROTC) program. She served as a platoon leader in Iraq and received a Bronze Star for her actions in rescuing another platoon that was coming under heavy enemy fire. When she completed her active-duty assignment, she was approached by another member of WATCH24 and offered a position. She told me she never gave it a second thought; she knew this was the career for her.

"Did you know your son has lost his interest in law enforcement as a career, but hopes to apply for a position in WATCH24 when he graduates from college next May," Sharon stated, not in the form of a question.

"Is that because of his fondness for you, or do you think he really wants that line of work?" I asked.

I could see Sharon's face turning a bit red as she replied, "I think he is truly interested in the work, but I suggested he may want to get some experience in the military or law enforcement before he applies. I hope you don't mind my suggesting that to him."

"Quite honestly," I went on, "he had previously expressed an interest in law enforcement or the military. Just like most other college students, I think he is still trying to find his way. Maybe all of this will give him some direction. It's time for me to sit down with him again and have a heart-to-heart discussion."

"I think he would like that," Sharon told me, "and I am quite fond of your son also. He is one of the nicest men I have ever met." I could see her blushing again.

"I will take that as a compliment to his parents," I said jokingly, and we both laughed.

Sharon knew her way around Washington DC. We went down several alleys as she quickly dialed her cell phone. "One minute," was all she said and after another two turns, she was at the rear door of the federal courthouse. The back door opened and an

FBI Agent and WATCH24 agent brought me from the car and into the building through the open door. It happened so quickly, I never had the chance to thank Sharon. Up three flights of stairs and I was led into a room with no windows where Jim and Tom were waiting with Steve Mason and a fourth man who I had not previously met.

Tom introduced all of us to Antonio Lopez, the FBI attorney who would be helping Steve with the presentation to the grand jury. As we sat down at a table, Jim updated us on his wife's condition, which had not changed. You could see the wear and tear all of this had on Jim, but he was here to make sure everything went as planned with the grand jury.

Steve began, "All three of you are going to testify before the grand jury this afternoon to lay out a clear picture for the jury of what is going on in this administration. I have found that grand juries can follow along much easier if Tony and I present the case in chronological order. So each of you will be before the grand jury at least twice today and I may need you tomorrow. Since we do not have all the evidence we require to place the President in the mix, I suggest that we never mention President Sanchez's name. The jury has the right to ask questions of the witnesses, and I am sure that at least one of them will bring up his name. Answer their questions as honestly as you can and do not hold back. Jim, you will be the first witness. I will need for you to explain why you thought you needed to create this group, how and why you chose the individual members and in general terms repeat that opening statement you gave us at our first meeting. Chuck, you will be next. I want you to lay out how Polk came to the White House, the two eavesdropping devices in your office and how you learned about Polk's meeting at the Mayflower. Make sure you emphasize that Cohn called you and lied about what Polk was doing that day. Then I am going to ask you to layout all the help you received from Steve Oates. Tom, you are next. You start by explaining the circumstances around Steve's death and why you believe it is a homicide. Then I will continue to relate the story to the grand jury, calling each of you back to the witness chair when I need your testimony. Jim, tomorrow I will need all the WATCH24 agents from the list we discussed yesterday and Tom, you will be in the witness chair for most of the early afternoon. The Judge told me he would extend the time to 7:00 p.m. both days so that we can finish in two days. Hopefully, it will not take the grand jury much time to come back with multiple indictments. Any questions?"

Jim spoke right away. "None for you Steve, but the three of us need to figure out a plan of action once you have the indictments."

Steve responded, "You have at least an hour now, while Tony and I get the grand jury sworn in, do the administrative briefing and warm them up for your testimony. In fact, please excuse us. We need to get going."

Once Steve and Tony left the room, we all agreed that probably the most critical step would be how and in what order we should execute the arrest warrants from the indictments and what order we should conduct the interrogations. These next steps will most certainly determine the tenure and future of President Sanchez.

"There is something you need to know about," Tom stated, interrupting my thoughts. "The Attorney General has ordered the United States Attorney from the Eastern District of Virginia to look into the death of Steve, the bombing at Chuck's house and the attempted murder of you, Jim. We have not released the fact that your wife was shot, but we will present that information to the grand jury. Let me say right up front that I do not trust him. He is a classmate and former law partner of the Attorney General. He will probably subpoena all the reports and since they are not on file, he will most certainly subpoena me. I hope this is just for show, but I can't be sure at this point."

"Do we have someone who can keep us posted on where this is heading?" I asked.

"I can tell you who visits his office, but that is about it," Tom replied.

Jim spoke, "Just keep us both in the loop. Hopefully our indictments will supersede anything he does."

We never finished our planning before Jim was called to the grand jury room. However, the way the conversation was heading, it looked like we were leaning toward arresting Polk first, since we still believed he is the weakest link and, quite candidly, cops generally do not do well under intense interrogation.

The afternoon seemed awfully long to me. Maybe confinement to a house in the middle of nowhere was not so bad after all. Jim was gone for over an hour and then I got my shot at it. I was in the witness chair for almost two hours and I felt it really went well. The jurors seemed genuinely interested and asked some good questions. It was 6:20 p.m. before I made my second trip to the grand jury room and 7:30 before we adjourned for the day. By the time I finished, Jim and Tom had left and Carol was there, ready to take me back to "my cabin in the woods." I was actually looking forward to a quiet night with my family.

"So, Carol, how did you get into this business?" I asked to open a conversation, hoping it would make the ride back to the house seem shorter.

"It is somewhat of a sad story with a happy ending," Carol began. "I am an Army brat; my father is a retired Colonel. I graduated from Duke University with a degree in psychology. I knew I wanted to do something that involved working with people, so I joined the Fairfax County Police Department having lived in Fairfax most of my life, since my father spent his last ten years in the Pentagon. I was single when I joined the Department, but got married three years later to one of the other patrol officers in my station. I transferred to another station since the Department had a policy against married officers working together. I did quite well and within eight years I was a Lieutenant in patrol. My husband struggled in his career because he did not have the discipline to study for promotional exams. I tried to help him, but he resented it and to make a long story short, he never advanced beyond patrol officer. He could never accept the fact that I out ranked him and he turned to alcohol which further damaged his career. We divorced and it got nasty. I just could not continue working with him and started looking to move to another police department. Every department I looked at would only accept me as a patrol officer, not as a Lieutenant. There is very little lateral movement in law enforcement. When the WATCH24 offer came, I jumped at it and here I am."

"Where's the happy ending?" I asked.

"That's the best part of the story," Carol went on. "I absolutely love my job. It is interesting, at times exciting and I get to meet and work with people like you and your family. And finally, last year I met a wonderful guy, who happens to be of all things, a doctor, and we are getting married next May. He generally knows what my job is and has a lot of respect for what we do. In fact, he has become the medical consultant for WATCH24 and if you or any member of your family became ill while you are with us, he would be the doctor that would provide the appropriate medical care."

"You are right; it does have a happy ending. Congratulations! I hope to meet him some day."

"I am sure you will, if not before, definitely next May," Carol said with a smile and a wink.

When we got back, Kim had a lovely dinner ready for the two of us. Everyone else had eaten and Tom, Marie and Sharon were all in the great room watching a college football game. I filled Kim in while we were eating, including the fact that there was no change in Patricia's condition. We went to bed early since Ben had told me that I needed to be ready to leave by 5:30 a.m. tomorrow morning to return to the courthouse. I was exhausted and looking forward to a full night's rest, and for a change, that is exactly what I had, without any middle of the night phone calls.

SATURDAY, SEPTEMBER 8

"Early to bed, early to rise" just isn't my style. I set the alarm for 4:30 a.m. and Kim had to get me up. I like routine. I know that is not a desired characteristic for anyone in law enforcement, but I am in the twilight of my career. I have been in the White House long enough to know what to expect every day. Of course, that was until the inauguration of President Robert Sanchez, who evidently follows no rules. So I would say that since I am indirectly responsible for the death of a fellow agent who was a great friend, I am living in the woods with my family, address unknown, because someone blew up my house, and I am getting up at 4:30 a.m. on a Saturday to sneak into the court house to testify against the President of the United States and his senior staff, my routine has been slightly interrupted. Life certainly can hand you some strange twists.

Sharon had breakfast waiting for me when I came out of the bedroom. I quietly ate trying to go over in my mind what I needed to cover today in the grand jury. Ten minutes later we were back in the car heading for Washington. Needless to say, traffic was much lighter on Saturday and we cut almost half an hour off the commute. Same drill as yesterday and to my surprise, I was the first one to the second floor conference witness room. This is a first; I hope nothing happened last night. My fears were put aside when Jim and Tom arrived with breakfast for six from McDonalds.

"Would you be disappointed if I told you I already had breakfast?" I asked.

"Not at all," quipped Jim, "I brought you lunch." It was always difficult to pull anything over on Jim. He looked much more rested today than yesterday. Having their daughter with Patricia gave Jim the occasional break he needed.

Before the others entered the room, Tom got up from his chair and locked the door. As he sat down, he stated, "The Vice President called my home last night and asked if he could talk to me in confidence. Naturally, I told him 'yes' and he then remained silent for a brief moment. 'I don't trust Cohn,' he stated. 'With all that is going on, I think the FBI needs to talk to him and see what he knows.' I then asked the Vice President if he or the President possessed any information that would help us in this investigation. He told me 'no' and told me to 'keep him up-to-date as the investigation progresses.' Rather strange, don't you think?"

"Real strange," Jim answered. "The problem for me is that I still can't figure out if he is involved in all of this. Needless to say, we won't tell him anything."

"I agree," I stated.

"I never planned on telling him anything," Tom stated. "I just wanted the both of you to know about the call and unless either of you see it differently, it stays with the three of us for now." We both agreed and Tom got up from his chair and unlocked the door. Steve and Tony arrived within a minute or so and we all started eating. I was surprised that I could eat again; I hope no one brings lunch today.

Steve and Tony thought everything went well yesterday and expected to finish today. I was first up this morning and walked to the witness chair at exactly 8:00 a.m. I picked up the story from a week ago Friday when the President called me to the Oval Office to relieve me of my assignment. I gave the jurors the word-for-word discussion as best I could remember. I continued with the bombing of my car and home and concluded with my being reunited with my family in a small home in the woods somewhere in Virginia. I was a little surprised when Steve handed me pictures of my car and home after the bombing and asked me to identify them the best I could. I paused and asked if I could have a minute or so to look over the pictures since this was the first time I had seen them. It suddenly dawned on me that was exactly the response Steve wanted. When I uttered, "Excuse the slight delay, but there is much more damage than I anticipated and it took me a second to orient myself," I noticed the instant smile on Steve's face.

As the day progressed, I met more of the WATCH24 agents

who not only guarded me, but saved my life. I immediately recognized one of them from our brief encounter on Pennsylvania Avenue over a week ago. I would be proud to have my son as part of this highly professional organization. Joe Wells and the General joined us by noon and it was good to see them. The General was excited to announce that he had obtained permission to actually give the sources of most of his intelligence information. Most CIA operatives felt they could not work for President Sanchez and would have to quit if he remained in office, so they were risking everything to see the President and his cronies get what they deserve.

The afternoon session moved rapidly and Steve announced he had completed the presentation at 5:25 p.m. Instead of adjourning for the evening, the grand jury saw the necessity of finishing today. By 6:30 p.m. the grand jury had returned indictments on Cohn, Polk, Martino, Del Toro and four Latino males involved in the bombing and attempted murder of Jim and the shooting of Patricia. Charges ranged from ethics and election law violations to money laundering, conspiracy to commit murder and several violations of the Racketeer Influence and Corrupt Organization (RICO) Act. Instead of dismissing the grand jury, Judge Walters adjourned it until further notice stating that he would reconvene the grand jury when there was more evidence to present.

There were a lot of handshakes and even more congratulations, especially to Steve and Tony for doing an outstanding job presenting the case and to Joe Wells for obtaining so much valuable information from the wires. Jim asked all of us to stay for a meeting of our group for an hour or so. Steve suggested that from here on, we exclude Judge Walters from our meetings since he will probably issue the arrest warrants and handle the arraignments probably issue the arrest warrants and handle the arraignments before he reassigns the cases. We all agreed.

Jim opened the meeting by thanking everyone for our patriotism, our outstanding work and the sacrifices that were made by all to get this far in such a short time. He told us that Patricia was showing some slight improvement today and thanked us for our prayers. He also thanked our families for all the hardships they endured as well. Then he cautioned us from thinking this case was almost over. There was still much work to be done. We still had to find those responsible for Steve Oates murder and we still did not have enough to impeach President Sanchez. Jim continued, "What I am suggesting now is the result of a lot of conversation with Chuck and Tom. I think it best if we arrest Cohn, Polk, Martino and Del Toro all at the same time, say 3:00 a.m. on Monday morning. We need to bring them to a single location where Tom, Chuck and I will do the interrogations. The others can be picked up starting at 6:00 AM Monday morning. The FBI will make the arrests and only record any spontaneous utterances from the defendants. Conversation with the defendants should be held to a minimum. No phone calls are to be made. Let me say that again, it is important that they not be allowed to make phone calls until we finish our interrogations. What does everyone think so far?"

Steve said, "Why not bring them directly here? They are going to be arraigned in the court room here, so that makes it easier for everyone."

Tom added, "We can do the processing here and that will keep it quiet until we are ready to release the information on the arrests. For the arrest part, I will send three agents to each address; I do not want anything going wrong."

the residences as well?"

"Based on the charges, I see no reason why we could not get them," Steve concluded. "I will see the Judge before he leaves."

Jim finalized everything by stating, "OK, Tom and I will take care of the logistics and make this work. I think it best that we should all be back here by 3:00 a.m. Monday morning.

"Concentrated power has always been the enemy of liberty."
—Ronald Reagan

CHAPTER 13

Sharon was waiting in the alley to take me back to the house in the woods. "I was expecting Carol," I said. "This is a very long day for you."

"I had four hours off this afternoon," Sharon told me, "and I volunteered to pick you up so I could talk to you."

"Sounds serious," I responded without thinking, "what's up?"

"More awkward than anything else," Sharon said sincerely. "Your son has asked me if we could date when this whole mess is over."

"And you don't want to hurt his feelings?" I asked.

"That's not it, I would like to go out with him, but I wanted to make sure it was OK with you and your wife," Sharon said without any hesitation.

I started laughing out loud and Sharon continued, "I graduated from college right after I turned 21 and there is less than a year between our ages."

"Sharon, I am not laughing about you two dating; I am laughing because you do not have to ask me if you two can date. In fact, I think it would be great. I knew from the time you two first met that Tom was taken by you. Trust me, Kim and I would be very happy if you and Tom got together."

"Thank you, sir," Sharon said with a smile.

"Don't let him break your heart," I said jokingly, "he has never had what I would call a long-term relationship."

"I know, he told me. How did it go today?" Sharon asked trying to change the subject.

"Good," I said. "You may have that date sooner than you think."

When I got back to the house, I immediately knew something was up. When I opened the door everyone yelled, "Congratulations!" "Jim called and gave us the good news," Kim stated. The table was all set for six with an extra plate on the counter, probably for the WATCH24 agent who would eat in the garage. In the middle of the table was a red, white and blue cake with six toothpick American flags on top. Kim, always the mother hen, said, "Everyone, wash up and sit down, dinner is getting cold." Carol made a plate and went to the garage so Ben could join us. Tom sat next to Sharon and they were all smiles. It was a wonderful dinner and although I commented that it was not over yet, the mood never changed. No one dared turn down a piece of the patriotic cake and we were just finishing our coffee when the phone rang. I quickly went to the bedroom to pick it up.

"Chuck, we have a little bump in the road," Tom Wilson began. "It appears that our wonderful Attorney General has orchestrated the issuance of arrest warrants for you, Jim, the Judge, the General and Steve. For whatever reason, he missed Joe Wells."

"What is the charge?" I asked.

"Attempting to Overthrow the Government," Tom replied. "The White House is preparing a press release as we speak. Watch the news at 11:00 a.m. and either Jim or I will be in touch later. I am not sure what this means, but we are working on it."

I sat on the bed for a moment to let what I just heard sink in. This was definitely not the way I wanted to end this mini celebration. The United States is in horrible shape if the Attorney General, the top law enforcement official in the country, is so corrupt that bogus arrest warrants are issued, and the Chief Justice is arrested. We are definitely at the point where the next 48 hours will determine whether the United States of America survives.

I returned to the table where there was silence as everyone's eyes followed me until I sat down. I told them exactly how Tom told me.

Kim and Marie teared up and Tom yelled, "Those bastards can't get away with this!"

Kim put her hand on Tom's shoulder and softly said, "Don't worry, they won't."

We had over an hour and a half before the 11:00 o'clock news. I switched the television to a college football game hoping that would help pass the time. It didn't. Kim, Marie and Sharon started cleaning up from dinner. Ben went to the garage to relieve Carol and Tom sat next to me on the couch to watch the game. He leaned over and in a very low voice said, "Thanks!" I winked and smiled knowing that he was referring to my earlier conversation with Sharon. I secretly hoped that his relationship with Sharon was long term, but I would never tell him. But then again, he had probably figured that out already.

You have no idea what it feels like to see your picture posted all over the news stating you are wanted by the FBI for attempting to overthrow the government. The news took everything from a press release from the Attorney General as gospel. It was "breaking news" on all the channels:

"There has been a strange twist to the stories we have been covering regarding the murder of a Secret Service Agent and the attempted murder of two federal law enforcement officials. According to a press release from the Office of the United States Attorney General, arrest warrants have been obtained charging six high ranking government officials with attempting to overthrow the Government of the United States. Both Charles R. Burke, former Secret Service Special Agent-in-Charge of the White House detail and James W. Bruce, former FBI Deputy Director, are among those being charged. According to the Attorney General, the bombing of Burke's vehicle and residence and the alleged attempted murder of Bruce were staged in order to avoid prosecution and allow them to escape the area. Also charged are Chief Justice John C. Walters, General J. Paul Monroe who served with the Joint Chiefs of Staff until his retirement, Steven Mason, retired United States Attorney from the Eastern District of Virginia and former White House Czar James Martino, who evidently was the inside person in the White House. Arrests are expected at any time. Even more astounding is the fact that the Attorney General believes that Burke and Bruce are also responsible for the death of Special Agent Steven Oates last week. The motive for that killing is unknown. The Attorney General has stated that he will be holding a full press conference on the case sometime Monday morning. Unnamed sources state that the investigation is being led by White House Special Agent-in-Charge Jeffrey Polk of the

Secret Service with assistance from the FBI. We will immediately bring you any additional breaking news on this story."

"Will the public actually believe this lie?" Tom asked.

"Most certainly," I replied, "the majority of the citizens have no idea what really goes on inside the Beltway."

"What happens now?" Kim asked.

"Nothing this evening," I told all of them, "but I need some sleep. Let's worry about this in the morning. I am sure Jim and Tom will have some sort of a solution by morning."

"Dad," started Marie, "how can you be so calm about this?"

"Two reasons, honey," I answered. "One, I can't do anything about it at 11:30 at night, and second, if you do what is absolutely right, you can only get into so much trouble. The truth will win every time! Let's see what the morning brings." And with that I headed for bed. If the truth be known, all I wanted to do is throw a set of handcuffs on Jeff Polk. I realized that I would not be the one who actually arrests him, but I will be the one who tells him he is going to prison for a long, long time.

What was most amazing is that Joe Wells somehow escaped being indicted. Had Steve Oates not discovered the eavesdropping devices in my office the day after we returned from Smith Mountain Lake, Cohn and Polk would have most certainly known that he was a member of our group. And if Joe's indictment had been made public with ours, I am not sure his wife would still be employed in the Sanchez Administration or he would still be happily married.

SUNDAY, SEPTEMBER 9

There was a slight knock on the door at about 1:30 a.m. according to my bedside clock. I quietly got up so I wouldn't wake Kim. "Sir," Ben said softly, "we have some activity on the perimeter. Can you come to the garage and please do not turn on any lights."

"I will be right there," I said. As I was getting dressed, Kim asked me what was going on. "I don't think it's anything, but stay in bed for now," I responded.

When I got to the garage, Ben and Carol were focused on two of the seven monitors. Ben motioned me over to where he was standing. "Look closely down the driveway about 400 feet. There is a pick up parked there with no lights on."

"I see it," I said.

"Now look at this monitor. There is a man standing next to this tree with a rifle."

"I do not see him, but is this the rifle right here?" I said pointing to the monitor.

"I believe so," said Ben, "and if you watch carefully, you will see some movement about four feet from the base of the tree."

"Got it," I said, but in reality I wasn't totally sure. "Where's Sharon?" I asked.

"She is out there lying in the brush hopefully with him in the crosshairs of her scope," Ben stated. "That's why I need you to help Carol monitor the cameras so I can stake out the guy in the truck."

"I can take care of that," I declared and Ben slipped out the side garage door.

"I don't see Ben or Sharon in any of the monitors," I told Carol after a few minutes.

"And you won't," Carol said softly, "they're pros at covert

surveillance."

Another 20 minutes passed and nothing but some slight movement from the man now sitting at the base of the tree. Suddenly, there was a short flash of light from the base of the tree. The radio clicked and I could hear Sharon in a low voice say, "Cigarette."

Carol started laughing. "These guys certainly can't be professionals;" I said, "what do you think they're doing?"

Carol said with a smile, "Probably jacking deer."

Ben came on the radio, "Sharon, if there is no activity for 30, give them a surprise Alpha at eleven."

"10-4" was Sharon's only response.

"I have been in law enforcement for a lot of years," I told Carol, "but I am not sure I know what that meant."

"That's because you do not do this often in your job. Twelve o'clock is due north. Sharon is at three o'clock in relation to her target. Ben wants her to go to eleven o'clock and set up a device to go off in 30 minutes that sounds like multiple gunfire. She will return to her three o'clock position before it goes off in case they decide to return gunfire. Ben chose 11 o'clock because there are open fields of fire and a hill at about 300 feet that would stop any bullets. This device is generally used to scare people away, so you can get back to bed. You may want to warn Kim, Tom and Marie so they don't think all hell is breaking loose. But, if they don't take off out of here, we may have a problem."

I quietly went to each bedroom and told Kim, Tom and Marie what was about to take place. Tom and Marie immediately went into their mother's room to keep her company and I returned to the garage.

The device did indeed sound like automatic weapon fire. The

subject by the tree ran as fast as he possibly could toward the pick up. The driver of the pickup spun the truck around and started heading down the driveway, slowing barely enough for the runner to jump into the bed of the pickup and off they went. Sharon and Ben were laughing out loud by the time they got to the garage. Ben's first words were, "Bedtime, sir, sorry we had to bother you."

I replied jokingly, "You couldn't have kept me away from this one. Thank you all and have a good night."

I went into the bedroom and told my family the whole story without leaving out any detail. We had a good laugh, which was needed, and by 3:30 a.m. we were all back in bed, with an agreement that no one would get up before nine. Usually, we would all get up to attend church together. Unfortunately, we could not take that risk today.

I am always the first one up in the morning; today I am last. No problem, I will just use that age old excuse: I must have needed the sleep. Kim, Tom and Marie were all at the breakfast table and were just finishing their breakfast. Kim had my plate ready and I sat down to eat as they all sat there and watched.

"OK, what's up?" I asked. "You are not all sitting here watching me eat unless you want something. So let's hear it."

"We need to do something different today," Kim started. "It's a beautiful day and we should be outside."

"Dad," Tom jumped in, "can we at least go for a hike in the woods or throw a football around outside?"

"Let me see what I can arrange," I answered with a smile. "Anything on the news this morning?"

"Nothing new; you're still a fugitive from justice," Marie said trying to bring a bit of levity into the conversation.

"And better a fugitive than an inmate," I quickly added. "By the way, where's the crew this morning?"

"Ben is in the garage and Carol and Sharon left early this morning," Tom told us.

After breakfast, I went to the garage to talk to Ben. "Anything exciting this morning?" I asked him.

"All quiet on the western front," Ben replied, "and we found a salt lick this morning in the woods, so they were looking for deer last night. I doubt they will return."

"I am sure they had to clean their pants after last night," I stated as we both laughed. "On a more serious note," I began, "Kim and the kids are getting a little restless staying inside. Anyway we can get them some fresh air today?"

"Let me see what I can do," Ben said with confidence. By the way he answered the question, I knew I didn't need to say anything else but "thanks."

Carol and Sharon returned about 11:00 o'clock. We were all sitting in the great room watching the Sunday morning news shows, when Sharon came in and announced, "All of you need to be ready to leave by noon for an afternoon picnic and that's all I am going to say for now." Everyone cheered and Marie said, "Thank you, Dad." I quickly realized that this outing had to be in the planning stage long before I spoke to Ben less than an hour ago.

It was a beautiful, warm, early fall day. Ben stayed behind while Carol and Sharon loaded us into a SUV and within 20 minutes we were in a secluded opening in the woods. Apparently it had been used before as a small camping area. There was a picnic table and a charcoal grill permanently mounted in a small concrete pad.

Carol laid down some rules so that there would be no doubt that WATCH24 was still responsible for our security. Tom and Sharon unloaded what looked like food for a dozen people and set up the table, while Carol set up some electronic equipment behind the SUV. Last to come from the back of the SUV was a softball and a football. Tom threw me a pass and we immediately went to the edge of the clearing so the football wouldn't interfere with any food preparation.

The meal consisted of hamburgers, hotdogs, baked beans, salad, chips and brownies for dessert. When you are in the great outdoors, it is difficult to find something that would taste any better than true American picnic-fare. In many ways, WATCH24 personnel were taking excellent care of all of us.

What amazed me is that despite being in the middle of what I considered to be the most serious emergency this country has faced in 200 years, we found time for a picnic. The Sabbath truly turned out to be just what the Lord intended—a day to rest and reflect.

We were back at the house by five. Ben told us that Tom Wilson had called to make sure we watched the 6:00 evening news. My best guess was that the White House has released a statement and it will be another lie that will upset all of us. I had almost an hour to wait, so I took a shower and changed my clothes so I would be ready for another dose of reality. I am really starting to wonder when there will be some sort of closure to this nightmare; to be honest, I am starting to lose my optimism.

The news opened with the anchor stating, "We have breaking news on the six high ranking officials charged with attempting to overthrow the government. For an update, we are live with Deputy

Director Thomas Wilson of the Federal Bureau of Investigation." Tom looked more confident than ever and made the following statement:

"Given the urgency and the serious threat to our country, the FBI has assigned an unusually high number of agents to this investigation. We currently have all the key players under surveillance and the public can expect that arrests will be made in the next 24 hours. The investigation will continue, and additional arrests are possible. I know that the public has many unanswered questions, so we have scheduled a press conference for tomorrow at 5:00 p.m. at which time we will be able to answer most of those concerns. Until then, we ask you for your patience."

I laughed out loud and everyone, who did not see the humor in Tom's statement, was staring at me. "Don't you see," I explained, "Tom has just set up the news media and the public for a big story about our arrests, but during the news conference, he will be announcing the arrests of Cohn, Polk and the others and the corruption in the Sanchez Administration. He will be dropping a bombshell that will shock the world. Talk about 'setting the stage.' This is brilliant."

As soon as the anchor moved to the next story, the phone rang. "So what did you think?" Jim asked.

"I thought it was brilliant," I said. "The news coverage will be worldwide."

"And that is exactly what we want," Jim added. "Remember, all of us will be meeting at 3:00 a.m. in the courthouse conference room in the morning, so make sure you get to bed early tonight," Jim reminded me.

"I am looking forward to it," I stated.

"We all are, see you in the morning," Jim said and hung up.

Sharon wanted to leave at 1:30 in the morning to head for the courthouse. If I skip breakfast here, I still had to be up by 1:00 a.m. at the latest, so I went to bed at 9:00 p.m. Unfortunately, I was understandably excited about finally being able to confront all these idiots and kept going over my interrogation plan. Consequently, I didn't actually fall asleep until after eleven.

"History records the successes of men with objectives and a sense

of direction. Oblivion is the position of small men overwhelmed by obstacles."

—William H. Danforth

CHAPTER 14

MONDAY, SEPTEMBER 10

By the time I got dressed and came out of the bedroom, Sharon had the coffee made and two travel mugs ready to fill. With less than two hours sleep, I wasn't very talkative in the car. After about ten minutes, Sharon said, "Why don't you catch a few winks; this may be your last chance for quite a long time." She was right and that is exactly what I did. Sharon was kind enough to wake me ten minutes before we arrived at the courthouse so I would look somewhat coherent.

Jim came through again. As I arrived, a catering service was setting up a breakfast buffet in the hallway outside the conference room. Jim insisted Sharon stay long enough to eat along with the other WATCH24 personnel and FBI agents. Fortunately, it appeared that not one of us had been arrested since everyone was present. I expected there would be a lively conversation given everything that happened and what was about to take place. However, there was very little conversation and no talk about the investigation. Then again when I thought about it, we were about to place a great scar on this nation; exposing unbelievable corruption resulting in the most substantial public distrust in our government since this country was founded. The aftermath of such an incident is unpredictable, but right now we had a lot of work to do to make sure our government can proceed with some form of integrity.

With a cup of coffee in front of each of us, Jim cleared the conference room so the eight of us—Jim, Tom, Judge Walters, General Monroe, Joe, Steve, Tony and I—could get down to business. Judge Walters told us he was working to relieve the Attorney General and other Justice Department officials of their duties until this investigation is complete.

Next, Tom put up a flip chart and started outlining what he hoped would take place this morning. "Cohn, Polk, Martino, and Del Toro are being arrested as we speak," Tom began, "and search warrants are being executed. I would expect that they will be arriving here about 4:00 a.m. Chuck, Tom and I will be doing the interrogations. If they want to talk, we will notify Steve or Tony who have equipment available to record their statements. Arraignment before Judge Walters is scheduled for 9:00 a.m. Any questions so far?" No one had a question. Knowing that the group would be discussing the specifics of the investigation, Judge Walters excused himself and left the room.

"I will be handling any evidence that the arrest teams have secured," Joe stated to the group. "If I think the evidence will assist you with your interrogations, I will let you know. If any statements are taken, I will secure those as evidence as well."

Steve spoke next. "I have some good news for you. At 6:30 a.m., Tony is appearing before a Federal District Judge to present a motion to dismiss the charges against all of us. I expect we will all be 'free men' before 7:00 a.m." Needless to say, everyone applauded. Steve continued, "Tony and I are scheduled to reconvene the grand jury at 10:00 this morning. Evidence will be presented that should result in the indictments of the Attorney General and several others from the Justice Department for their lying before the court and bringing false charges against us."

"Two last items," Tom concluded. "We still do not know or have any concrete details on whether this group has actually been able to bring any nuclear devices into the country. If one of the defendants does agree to talk, General Monroe and I will do the questioning in that area. Second, we do not know how wide the corruption is in the White House or beyond. Any information we obtain today will be presented to the grand jury later in the week. Steve will let us know the date and time."

Jim was the last to speak before we went about our tasks. "It was 22 long days ago that we first met in Fredericksburg and we began this mission to save our country. Unfortunately, we lost Steve Oates along the way and Patricia was seriously injured. She is recovering, but it will take some time, so please keep her in your prayers.

But somehow, through the grace of God, all of the rest of us survived and today we sit here ready to bring law and order back to our great nation. Isn't it ironic that tomorrow is September

11th? However, our work is not complete, our mission is not yet accomplished, and we are still not sure if we have enough evidence to remove President Sanchez. But the truth is that we did make a difference and I am so proud of all of you. I said it before and I will say it again. All of you are true patriots. Let's go and finish our job!"

Cohn was the first to be brought in. He was in a pair of jeans and a tee shirt and was unshaven. Quite frankly, he looked like any other criminal coming through the door in handcuffs. Now that I think about it, that is exactly what he is. Once he was placed in a room, Jim, Tom and I entered. He looked directly at me and as cocky as ever said, "So you are still alive."

"In spite of your efforts," was my reply.

He put his head down and said nothing else. Tom asked him if he understood the charges. He looked up again and stated, "You are looking at the wrong guy; you need to talk to Martino. That's all I am going to say and I want my lawyer."

I sat down in the chair next to him and in a very calm voice said, "Mr. Cohn, you do not have to say a word and we will not ask any questions. But when your attorney gets here, I want you to tell him exactly what I am about to tell you. You may have bugged my office, illegally I might add, but we have had a court interception on a number of phones to include yours. We executed a search warrant on your townhouse and seized a briefcase containing the $2 million from the exchange in the Mayflower. We have a number of people under arrest including the two who placed a bomb in my car. Polk, Martino and Del Toro have also been arrested this morning. One or more of them will talk. With the death of Steve Oates and three attempted murders, everyone is looking at life as a minimum sentence. I am sure you know how this works. The first person to talk gets the deal. You are the first person we are talking to this morning. I really do not care if you talk; quite honestly, I am glad you do not want to talk to us. But let me assure you, one of the others will help himself out and talk to us this morning. We have the evidence to convict despite what happens this morning. We will be requesting that all of you be held without bail, so your last full day as a free man was yesterday. And by the way, the federal prison system is filled with inmates who have committed some of the worst crimes known to man. But strangely enough, most of them are very patriotic and will not be your friend. I hope you enjoy the rest of your day; I know I will."

Somehow saying that gave me a great deal of satisfaction. The three of us walked out of the room leaving Cohn with the FBI agent guarding him.

"He's nervous as hell," Tom said as we sat down in the conference room. "And I think that if we really need his cooperation, we should give it another shot."

"I agree," Jim replied, "but let's hold off and see what happens with the other three."

Orlando Del Toro was the next through the door. As we started toward the room to begin our interrogation, we were stopped by Joe Wells.

"FYI," Joe told us, "the agents found two handguns and $50,000 in twenties in Del Toro's apartment."

"Thanks, Joe, that gives us something to talk about in there," Jim responded.

Jim began before we sat down. "Orlando, looks like you got in over your head this time. But before we go any further, let me tell you your Constitutional rights as a visitor to this great nation of ours." Jim actually took a card from his wallet and very slowly and with exact pronunciation read Del Toro his rights.

"I know my rights, I've heard them before," Del Toro responded, "and I want a public defender."

"We will start working on getting you a lawyer," Jim told him. "But it appears you have some problems that even your drug cartel pals from Mexico can't help you with. You see we have the two handguns from your apartment, and we will be checking to see where they came from and if the bullets match any of our open cases. That charge is a felony. Then there's the 50 grand in cash. We need to find out where that came from, although we think we already know. You will be charged with that as well. Then there is the homicide of Secret Service Agent Steven Oates, the bombing of Mr. Burke's car and the attempted murder of yours truly. Add that to the five or six murders that you committed in Mexico and you can probably begin to understand your dilemma. It looks like you will be spending the remainder of your life in a federal prison if you are not executed. By the way, if you think President Sanchez is going to help you, forget it. You see, he also has some problems which are quite similar to yours. So, what I am telling you Orlando is that you do not have to tell us anything. But there is only one person that can help you now, and that is you. Think it over and I will come back to check on you in a while."

We left the room and Tom was the first to speak. "Del Toro has nothing to gain by talking. He is heavily involved in all of this and I expect the $50,000 was payment for either the bombing or the attempted murder of you, Jim. My best guess is that the guns will come back stolen, but not linked to any crimes here. I think we need to check with Mexican authorities also."

"I say we ignore him and let his attorney approach us," I said, "We do not need his testimony."

Jim agreed and added, "We still need evidence to implicate the President. There is no doubt in my mind that he knew everything that took place and I consider the case incomplete until he is charged and convicted criminally."

It was now 4:30 a.m. and two FBI agents brought Polk up the stairs and into another vacant office. One of the FBI agents came back out of the room and said to me, "Sir, we took his badge, ID and service weapon and gave them to Mr. Wells for safekeeping. We also seized his day timer which you may want to look at before you talk to him."

"Thanks, we will," I replied. As I started out the door, seeking Joe, he was walking toward our room.

We all sat down, and Joe opened Polk's day timer. "Polk kept good notes on all his meetings with everyone, including you Chuck," Joe began. "He has some cryptic notes for each meeting which may be incriminating. You may want to take some time to review it before your interrogation."

"Thanks, Joe," Tom said, "I am the lead on this one and this may be the break we need."

We spent the next 15 minutes reviewing Polk's day timer. It was interesting. On September 4th, the morning of the car bombing, Cohn, Polk and Martino met with President Sanchez at 8:30 a.m. There was a plus sign encircled on that date. On September 5th, the day of the attempted murder of Jim, the same group met at 8:00 a.m. and the day timer had a minus sign encircled on that day. Also of interest were two other meetings, one at 7:00 p.m. on the 5th and one at 9:00 in the morning of the 6th. President Sanchez, the Attorney General, Cohn and Polk were present for both of those meetings. This time the capital letter "I" was encircled which I guessed meant indictments.

Tom smiled and stated, "Polk's training to keep good notes just screwed him and probably made our case against the President."

"He will fold," Jim concluded. "I have found through experience that cops have a difficult time during criminal interrogations and more often than not, usually confess."

"I have said all along that Polk would be the weak link," I added.

When we walked into the room, Polk's eyes opened wide. He looked like a deer caught in the headlights of a car. We sat down and Polk spoke up immediately. "I know you are not going to believe this, but I am glad to see you two alive."

Tom sat there flipping through the pages of Polk's day timer, not saying a word. I did not think it possible, but Polk's eyes opened wider and then his head fell and he stared at the floor. Tom waited another few minutes and then introduced himself.

Polk stopped him and said, "I know who you are and I am going to save you some time. I want my attorney here as soon as possible. Give me 15 minutes with him and I will tell you everything—no bullshit, no lies— everything."

I was shocked he folded so easily. I couldn't help myself thinking that the end could be in sight.

"Jeff," I said, "one question. President Sanchez..."

"He knew everything and directed everything," Polk blurted and started to cry. "I haven't been right since Steve was killed," he said through his tears. The three of us quietly left the room as Polk continued to sob.

"How in the hell did a Secret Service agent like Jeff get caught up in a mess of this magnitude?" I said rhetorically.

"I guess the President has much more charisma than we give him credit for and Polk was in awe of him. Under those circumstances, some people just lose their moral compass," Tom responded.

"We will soon get an answer to your question, Chuck," Jim said as a matter of fact.

We needed a break, so we each grabbed a cup of coffee and a bagel and returned to our conference room. Martino had been placed in another room while we were in with Polk. "Let him sit awhile; it will do him good," Jim surmised. We went over all we had learned this morning and concluded that we had enough to visit the President later this morning.

Not one of us expected to get anything out of Martino since he had a criminal record and had been through this drill numerous times before today. He actually smiled as we walked through the door. "Greetings gentlemen; have a seat," Martino said being a wise ass. "What can I do for you today?"

"You can listen while we explain the charges against you," Tom said. Tom read the indictments to him and he showed absolutely no emotion whatsoever.

Again, I could not help myself and added, "And the Attorney General, at the direction of the President, has also charged you with treason for attempting to overthrow the government."

Martino exploded. "Why that dirty lying son-of-a-bitch," Martino shouted, "I was helping him save this country and they charge me with treason. Those bastards. I have gotten them over $20 million. I did everything they asked me to do, and they say I was trying to overthrow the government. I'll show them. What do you want to know?"

Now it was our eyes that were wide open. We did not see this coming. Tom asked me to get either Steve or Tony and have one of them come in with a recorder. As I walked out of the room, Jim followed. Once in the hallway, Jim slapped me on the back and stated, "That was a great move, Chuck, you just broke this case wide open. Let's get back in there before he changes his mind."

With Steve present and the recorder on, Martino was given his rights by Tom who carefully explained each one. Martino was so anxious it appeared he could not wait to tell his story. He started by telling us he has known President Robert Sanchez for years, long before he ran for President. Martino had arranged anywhere between $10,000 and $50,000 "donations" for Sanchez's campaigns from the start of his political career, mostly through the Mexican drug cartels. When Sanchez decided to run for President, he approached Martino and asked what it would take to get much larger donations. Martino told him the cartel wanted less enforcement on the border and, for his part, Martino wanted to work in the White House. The deal was struck and Sanchez was elected President. During the campaign, Martino met Polk while Sanchez was campaigning in the El Paso area. Martino started calling Polk and giving him information on some of the renegade Mexican drug dealers. Polk started to get recognition for providing information that led to more arrests and seizures in the El Paso field Office and Martino began eliminating the cartel's competition. Polk never officially listed Martino as an informant, and they developed a working relationship.

The cartel continued sending money as long as the border enforcement was limited. Cohn had approached Martino and told him the President needed a couple of packages delivered to the United States undetected through the border. Martino assured him they could easily take care of it and two packages came through the border that Martino knew about. He claimed he did not know for sure what they were, but expected that it was something illegal so he did not ask any questions.

According to Martino, everything was going fine until the exchange of money at the Mayflower. Once the administration realized that they were being watched, the President had a meeting with Cohn, Polk and Martino and told them to eliminate the problem without involving the White House. Martino knew he would be a hero to President Sanchez if Jim and I were somehow "eliminated." And Martino knew that Del Toro had the people who could handle the "assignments." However, Del Toro himself was the one who shot and killed Agent Oates at the request of Cohn. Martino said he got upset that Del Toro did it himself, because he could be easily linked to him. So Del Toro brought in some of the cartel henchmen from El Paso for the bombing and attempted murder of Jim. President Sanchez was updated regularly by Cohn and meetings were held to discuss any additional assignments. Once the White House found out that Jim and I were still alive and in hiding, all operations ceased. Obviously, Martino did not know that President Sanchez was laying all of this on him.

After Martino's statement, Jim got the entire group together except for Judge Walters. Jim brought everyone up to speed on everything that occurred this morning so far. He also requested that the defendants be kept apart until after their arraignment. Then he stated, "I am afraid, gentlemen, that our worst fear may have come true. According to Martino, the President and Cohn had at least two unknown packages brought into the country through the Mexican border. There is a distinct possibility that these packages may be dirty bombs. Hopefully, Polk may know more about these packages, but we will have to wait and see."

"Jim, let me call my sources and see what I can find out," General Monroe said. "Any idea on the date they may have entered the States?"

"I will see if we can get you some dates, General," Jim told him.

"Before we start getting lawyers in here and word of the arrests starts to spread, Chuck, Tom and I are going to the White House to have a talk with the President," Jim told everyone. "I will let you know how we do."

On the way to the White House, I glanced at my watch; it was 6:20 a.m. I called ahead and was hoping I would know the agent that answered the phone.

"Agent Wright," he said as he picked up the phone.

"Dennis," I said, "listen closely. This is Special Agent-in-Charge Charles Burke. How are you? "

"I am fine, sir. How are you?" Wright responded somewhat surprised.

"I am fine Dennis. I want you to call upstairs and tell the President that Mr. Cohn needs to see him in the Oval Office in 15 minutes. Do not tell anyone you talked to me. Do you understand?"

"Yes sir," he said.

"Good," I said, "meet me in about five minutes just outside the Oval Office for further instructions."

"Yes, sir. I will be there and it's great to hear from you," Wright said with a bit of excitement in his voice. Both Tom and Jim laughed. "Nothing like the element of surprise," I said with a smile.

Getting into the White House with my emergency bypass card that I still had was not difficult and this certainly was an emergency. Agent Wright was right there waiting for us. I explained to Dennis that we were no longer wanted and the charges were bogus.

"I knew that, sir," he said.

I also told him that there were going to be some changes around the White House to which he smiled and replied, "About time!"

He led us into the Oval Office and was instructed not to say anything to the President except "Good morning" and to stand outside the Oval Office.

"I will be right here if you need me, sir," he told me and as he left we each took a chair in front of the President's desk.

"Experience hath shown that even under the best forms of government those entrusted with power have, in time, and by slow operations, perverted it into tyranny."
—Thomas Jefferson

CHAPTER 15

President Sanchez walked into the Oval Office with his usual air of arrogance and had the surprise of his life. We all stood up out of respect for the position, not the man. "Good morning, Mr. President," we all said in unison. The look on his face was one of pure shock. He stopped dead in his stride and after a brief pause yelled, "Agent, get in here right away! Arrest these men," he told Wright as he came through the door.

"No sir, Mr. President," Wright said with great satisfaction, "they did not commit any crime and they are not wanted."

"It's true Mr. President," I said. "The charges were dismissed this morning. Why don't you sit down and we can discuss all of this." The President turned his back to us and seemed to be staring out his window. He suddenly turned and angrily yelled, "Where's

Cohn?"

"He was arrested this morning on a number of indictments and currently is in custody of the FBI," I told him. He reluctantly sat behind his desk and Agent Wright left the Oval Office. The President just sat there, not knowing what to say. Finally he asked in a more civil tone, "Why wasn't I notified about all of this?"

"That's why we are here," Jim stated. "Polk, Martino and Del Toro are also under arrest and in custody," Jim added. The President sunk in his chair.

"Before you say anything Mr. President let me explain," I began. "We have all the evidence we need to put all of them away for life, if they do not get the death penalty which is allowed under federal law. And by the way, they are talking. We also have enough evidence to put you away for life, Mr. President. And I wouldn't be calling the Attorney General for any advice. He and several of his cronies will be indicted later this morning."

The President just sat there for several minutes. Finally he spoke. "I am sure you have a reason for being here other than to bust my balls and watch me squirm."

Jim spoke up immediately. "Mr. President, we also know you and Cohn had several packages covertly brought into the country through the Mexican border. Intelligence sources tell us they are dirty bombs. You would be doing yourself a very large favor if we had enough information to seize these bombs before a large number of citizens are killed or injured."

The President sat there for another long period of time, apparently deep in thought. Finally, he asked another question. "Have you notified Congress yet?"

Tom responded, "The FBI has a meeting scheduled with the leadership at 10:30 a.m. and a press conference scheduled for noon. I imagine Congress will start impeachment proceedings immediately."

The President rose from his chair and said, "If you would excuse me, I have some important decisions to make." He then walked out of the room without another word.

"I guess an apology is out of the question," I said in order to give some levity to the situation.

The conversation on the short trip back to the court house was all about President Sanchez and what he would do. We all agreed that his only option was resignation. However, he was in a bind if he wanted a deal of no criminal prosecution in return for his resignation. The Attorney General was in no position to offer that type of deal. The Vice President could give him a pardon, but we believe the American people would not stand for that and such a move would certainly end the Vice President's political career. And quite honestly, we are not yet sure if the VP is involved in any or all of this or if he even knew about it. Right now he appears clean. But the more important question concerned the dirty bombs. Does President Sanchez know where those bombs are presently located? If he does, will he somehow get that information to the FBI? If he does not, who does? Perhaps Polk can help us locate the bombs. Cohn probably knows, but none of us think he will talk.

Now that the President knew what had taken place this morning, all the defendants were allowed to make calls to their lawyers and family. To no one's surprise, Cohn called the Attorney General at home. To Cohn's surprise, the Attorney General told him that he would have to find a private attorney to represent him. Polk, on the other hand, must have expected something. According to the agent guarding him, Polk opened his wallet, took any change in attitude. An attorney from the Public Defender's Office had arrived and the agent was outside the room so as to not interfere with the attorney/client conversation. Jim knocked on the door and opened it slightly. The attorney motioned us to come in and stated, "My client has chosen not to say anything at this time. After I see the evidence you have against him, I may decide that Mr. Del Toro can help you with the cases against the other defendants."

"That's fine," Jim said, "but you are about an hour too late counselor. We do not need Mr. Del Toro's assistance. Have a wonderful day." With that, we walked out of the room.

It was about 15 minutes before Polk's attorney arrived and we gave them 20 minutes together, five minutes more than Polk originally requested. I knocked on the door, opened it and the three of us walked into the room. "Are you ready for us?" Tom asked.

"We are," the attorney said. He then asked, "Can we record this conversation so I can have a copy and there is no misunderstanding?"

"No problem," Tom replied and opened the door. Steve walked in carrying the digital recording equipment.

There was no doubt that Polk was extremely emotional and full of remorse. I expected him to come around, but I did not expect the changes I was seeing. Polk went from a self assured, somewhat cocky Secret Service supervisor to a defeated, insecure, emotional defendant confused as to how he ended up with handcuffs on his wrists. What a tragedy, I thought, what a tragedy.

Polk began explaining his relationship with James Martino in El Paso very much in the same way Martino related it. It was out a folded piece of paper, dialed the phone and immediately began speaking to an attorney.

Jim and I first went back to Del Toro's room to see if he had Martino who asked him if he would be interested in a supervisory position in the White House, which was completely outside the normal promotional process of the Secret Service. At this stage, Polk had committed several administrative violations regarding informants, but nothing criminal and in fact, nothing that would have cost him his job. Apparently, that all changed very quickly after his arrival at the White House. Cohn asked him if he could unofficially and covertly place a listening device in a vacant office. Polk told us he hired a private investigator to do the job and paid him out of his own pocket in order to gain favor from Cohn and the President. When Cohn moved me to that office, Cohn asked Polk to monitor the device and let Cohn know if anything unusual occurred. Polk never questioned Cohn as to the reason for the device and knew at that time that it was unlawful. The result was that the President, Cohn and Polk all knew about our group and the calls back and forth to Steve Oates.

Polk continued stating that he was ordered by Cohn to go to the Mayflower to ensure there was not a problem. He knew there was an exchange of money, but he was told it was a CIA operation and the White House could not trust me, the Secret Service SAC, to know anything about it.

Tom stopped him and asked, "So Jeff, what you are saying is that you did everything that Cohn or the President asked of you?"

"Yes sir," Polk replied.

"What did they ask you to do about Agent Oates?" Tom asked.

Polk began to sob again. "They asked me for his home address,"

Polk said softly through his tears. "I didn't know they were going to kill him. When I heard of his death, I got upset and went to the President because Cohn wasn't in his office. The President told me that this was a matter of national security and it was being controlled at the highest levels of the CIA and FBI. Unfortunately, I took the President at his word."

"So indirectly, you were responsible for the murder of a fellow Secret Service Agent." It was a statement I made out of anger and not a question. Polk just slowly nodded his head, acknowledging I was right.

Polk went on. "The next day the President called me into the Oval Office. When I arrived, Cohn and Martino were already there. The President first told me that Special Agent-in-Charge Burke was going to be replaced because he had passed some top secret material to an opposing political organization. He then told me I would be promoted to the SAC position. Needless to say, I was on cloud nine thinking that the President and Cohn had full trust in me." Polk turned to me and said, "But when I heard that you were killed by a bomb placed in your car, I started to realize that I was being used. I began to make cryptic notes in my day timer just in case I was right. I should have gone to the Director or to the FBI, but I did nothing. The President and Cohn kept assuring me that this was the largest espionage case this country has ever experienced and that I needed to do my job and not worry about it. I did not believe them, but I did not know where to turn."

Tom took out Polk's day timer and started flipping through it. Finally he asked Polk, "What did the plus sign on the meeting of the 4th mean to you?"

"That was the mood of the meeting," Polk answered. "Even though we all thought Mr. Burke was dead, the three of them seemed happy."

"Then I am assuming that the minus sign posted with the meeting the morning they tried to murder Mr. Bruce was because they were sad?"

"Exactly," Polk replied, "and the letter 'I' means indictments of Mr. Bruce's group because I could not get a good read on their mood. They seemed concerned. Since the Attorney General was present, I started to think that the President and Cohn may have been telling me the truth all along. I guess I should have paid attention to my first instincts."

"One more question, Jeff," Tom stated. "Do you know anything about several dirty bombs or material for dirty bombs being brought into the States through the Mexican border?"

"This is the first time I heard of that, sir," Polk said.

"That's what I thought," Jim sighed obviously frustrated with the lack of information on the bombs.

Last on our list was one more attempt with Cohn and we only had one question for him. Tom asked General Monroe to join us and we all went into the room and sat down. Cohn's attorney jumped to his feet and actually yelled, "You are not to question my client!"

"Relax counselor," Tom said, "we are not here to ask questions; we are here just to give you important information. We have reason to believe that several dirty bombs were brought into this country at the direction of the President and Mr. Cohn. We don't care how we find out or who tells us, but for the sake of this country and the safety of all Americans, we need to know where these bombs are located. If we do not find them and something happens, the two of you will have to bear that burden."

There was a long pause where not a word was spoken. Cohn

looked worse than words could possibly describe. Finally, he spoke. "I have no idea what you are talking about; you will have to ask the President."

The General just stared at Cohn for at least three minutes. Everyone in the room was getting uncomfortable and the General knew it. Although I had not known him personally for a very long period of time, I knew the man. I had never seen the General this upset. With a slightly reddened face, he began to lecture Cohn. "Son, I hope you do not believe that you are patriotic or even a decent man. I have spent my entire adult life protecting my country from foreign enemies never expecting to find an enemy as despicable as you within our own borders. You are no better than Osama bin Laden; in fact you are worse because you are plotting to kill your fellow citizens."

The General then left the room, so I got up and also left the room, with Tom and Jim in toe.

"He's a lying son-of-a-bitch," Jim said loudly.

"Just like his boss," I added. There were no laughs this time.

"If anything is worthy of a man's best and hardest effort, that

thing is the utterance of what he believes to be the truth."
—Edwin Arlington Robinson

CHAPTER 16

We were all there for the court proceedings. The five of us, General Monroe, Joe, Tom, Jim and I sat together in the front row with Steve and Tony seated at the table in front of us and the defendants and their attorneys to their left. The courtroom was filled with FBI agents and many of the WATCH24 personnel who have been protecting us. I saw Sharon smile as I looked toward her.

Judge Walters began the arraignment with a statement to all the defendants and their attorneys:

"Today is both a sad day and a wonderful day for our great nation. Our forefathers had the intelligence and the foresight to bring law and order to this newly formed country through a magnificent document called the Constitution of the United States of America. The Constitution protects the citizens of America, not the government. One way the Constitution guarantees this protection is through the separation of the powers of the federal government by the creation of three branches— the Executive Branch, which is the Office of the President, the Legislative Branch, which is our Congress and the Judicial Branch, which includes all the judges. I am saddened today because the Executive Branch is accused of ignoring the Constitution so they could illegally expand and abuse their powers for personal gain. When their actions were brought into question, they resorted to the murder of law enforcement officers. I am encouraged today because our Constitution is a living document and under its rules, those charged with these disgraceful, hideous crimes will be tried in a court of law."

Judge Walters then began the arraignments of President Sanchez's senior staff. One by one they stood before the Judge. Cohn, Martino and Del Toro all pled, "Not Guilty" and were held with no bail. Polk tried to plead "Guilty," but the Judge would not accept it, changed his plea to "Not Guilty" and held him without bail as well, telling him he could enter a guilty plea at his next court appearance.

I could actually feel some relief in my entire body. If only President Sanchez would somehow let us know the location of the dirty bombs, the end of this nightmare could be in sight.

Once the defendants left the courtroom, Judge Walters came down from the bench and stood before the seven of us and smiled. He then spoke to everyone that was present.

"I have been on the bench for over 30 years," he began, "and I have to tell you, I have never experienced the feelings I am having at this moment. We all have been through much turmoil and heartache over the last several weeks, and yet here we stand together, not basking in our glory, but counting our blessing that our country has survived this despicable attempt to tarnish our Constitution and destroy our republic. Today will go down in history, but few will remember the real heroes of today. Many of them are in this room. I am proud of each one of you for having the courage to stand up and do what is right. May God continue to bless you and the United States of America."

And with those words, Judge Walters shook the hand of everyone in the room and left the courtroom.

The grand jury went as expected with a second series of indictments on the Attorney General and two others from his office for falsifying the court records on the indictments for attempting to overthrow the government. The FBI immediately executed the warrants and arraignment was set for 1:00 p.m. this afternoon. To put it mildly, the Attorney General went kicking and screaming, stating that he would be vindicated and those who were responsible for his indictment would pay.

Tom wanted all of us to stick around for the midday press release and conference. I would rather go back to my cabin in the woods and get some sleep. However, everyone else was going to be there, so I said I would be there with "the team." We were all sitting in our conference room waiting to go over the final version when Tom's cell phone rang. We were silent so Tom could hear, but I knew something was wrong by the look on his face and the change in his color. He hung up the phone, put it away and looked at all of us. "Just when you think this case cannot get any more bizarre, it takes another strange twist," he told us. "President Sanchez just committed suicide inside the White House."

We all sat there in shock, not saying a word. I spoke first, "How?"

"Gunshot to the head," Tom replied.

"Are we sure it is a suicide?" Jim asked.

Tom answered, "He was in a locked bedroom, no one else present. It appears to be a suicide."

"That no good bastard!" General Monroe said rather loudly. "He must really hate our country. He could possibly be our only hope of recovering those dirty bombs and he takes his own life. It was a selfish, cowardly act with no regard for the lives of others."

"Perhaps he had a plan in place for their detonation and he knew he could not stop it," I added, "Any suicide note?"

"Not that I know of," Tom told us.

Jim stood up and said, "General, Chuck, Tom, let's go tell Cohn the bad news and see if that opens him up. He is our last hope to get any information on the bombs."

We got back to the room where Cohn was being held just in time. Two United States Marshals were ready to take him to one of the local jails. We asked for five minutes and they left the room.

"What do you want now?" Cohn questioned sarcastically.

Jim was the first to speak. "Stewart, we have some bad news for you. President Sanchez just committed suicide in the White House."

"You're lying, trying to get me to talk," said Cohn, who suddenly seemed very emotional.

"He's telling you the truth," I told him. Cohn lost it. He started sobbing uncontrollably and his body began to shiver. I am not sure if it was out of his love for the President or if he now realized that any chance for getting out of this with a presidential pardon just went down the sewer.

We said nothing for almost ten minutes and finally, Tom broke the silence. "Stewart, this country is in grave danger unless we recover those dirty bombs. You are the only one that can do what's right and tell us how we can recover them."

Cohn just sat there. "This may be your only chance to save your ass from execution," Jim spat angrily in an attempt to get Cohn to open up.

"I told you before, I do not know how to locate them and I can't help you," Cohn stated emphatically through his tears. The three of us left the room and told the Marshals to go ahead and take him to jail.

We returned to the conference room where the remainder of our group was anxiously waiting, hoping for some good news. Before he sat down, Jim said, "He still says he knows nothing and can't help us locate the dirty bombs." I watched as everyone sunk in their chairs.

"What's next?" Joe Wells asked.

"I wish I knew," Tom replied, "I wish I knew!"

Needless to say, with the President's death, our press conference was canceled and changed to a press release only. Now the Vice President was to give a news conference right after he was sworn in as President. Tom would be in attendance to answer any questions that the press would have regarding the investigation and arrests. The main concern, and rightfully so, was to keep the nation calm and show the country that our Constitution ensures a smooth transition of power during a crisis. For now, at least, the information on the dirty bombs was to remain classified and kept from the American people.

Sharon was somewhat excited about all that took place today, and on the trip back to the house in the woods, she told me how proud she was that we had saved our country. "You were just as much a part of it as we were," I told her.

"Not really," she responded, "but I am glad I was involved in all of this. This is probably the most important national event I will ever witness in my lifetime."

"I certainly hope so," I said still thinking of those dirty bombs somewhere in our country.

I could feel myself falling asleep and I just let it go. By the time I woke up, we were in the driveway and my family was standing outside the car anxiously waiting. I received the warmest reception any man could wish for by a very happy and relieved family. "It's over," I said knowing that was not true. Kim and Marie cried tears of joy, Tom hugged Sharon and her kissing him on the cheek did not go unnoticed. They all told me how proud they were of me and the entire team. Ben and Carol joined us briefly, congratulating me and shaking my hand. It was a wonderful homecoming and one I will never forget.

Kim had an early dinner waiting for us and the four of us sat down to eat. We had just said grace and begun eating when Ben and Carol came into the kitchen. "So where do we go from here?" I asked Ben.

"Actually, no place right now," Ben said to all of our surprise. "Let's give it a couple of days to make certain we have all the key players locked up and no nuts surface who are seeking revenge for the death of the President. Besides, you won't be able to move back into your house for several months. If everything is still calm by Wednesday, we will take another look at returning to some sense of normalcy."

"I think that's a good idea," said Kim, the proverbial mother hen. To be honest, now that I think about it, I also believe it is a good idea.

Every television station had continuous coverage on the death of President Sanchez. As far as the investigation went, Tom did an outstanding job summarizing the case and he gave the team full credit by name. He even stated that our team had nearly completed the investigation and then sought help from the FBI. All the stations had pictures of all of us, to include Steve Oates and labeled us the "heroes" who saved our country. But to me, the best part was the rhetorical questions asked by one of the cable networks:

How did we let this happen to our country and why did only seven men have the courage to do something about it? What changes need to be made in our federal government to prevent anything like this from happening again?

Since I had been operating for the past 18 hours on little sleep and sheer adrenaline, the evening was short for me and both Kim and I headed for the bedroom at about 9:00 p.m. We got ready for bed and as I turned off the light I said, "I don't think we have to worry about any calls in the middle of the night." Kim laughed slightly and said, "Don't be too sure!"

"The courage of life is often a less dramatic spectacle than the

courage of a final moment, but it is no less than a magnificent mixture of triumph and tragedy. People do what they must—in spite of personal consequences, in spite of obstacles and dangers and pressures—and that is the basis of all human morality."
—John F. Kennedy

CHAPTER 17

SATURDAY, DECEMBER 22

It has been over three months since the arrests. One of Del Toro's handguns matched the bullets in the Steve Oates' homicide and the new United States Attorney General, Steven Mason, stated he would be seeking the death penalty for Del Toro and the other three defendants who were involved in the vehicle bombing and the attempted murder of Jim and Patricia Bruce. Both Jeffrey Polk and James Martino have entered guilty pleas and agreed to testify in the trials of all the other defendants.

Tonight Jim hosted the WATCH24 Christmas party and he had invited all the team members and their families. Patricia had recovered enough from the shooting to attend in a wheelchair. Jim was working from home now and rarely left her alone, so I knew that everything was much better between them. Actually so much so, Patricia asked me to take Jim to lunch once in a while to give her a break.

It was very much like a reunion of everyone involved in the case. Jim was able to convince Joe Wells to join WATCH24, which by the way, is now the premier security company in the world. General Monroe is now Chairman of the Board for WATCH24. Kim and I really enjoyed the party and it is our first chance to relax since moving back into our home ten days ago. Kim has returned to her teaching job and still plans to retire a year from June. Tom and Marie went back to school and in spite of the interruption, they both did well this past semester. Tom will be graduating in May and has decided to join the FBI. He and Sharon are still an item and I expect they will be married within the year. I returned to my position as head of the White House Detail. Several weeks after I returned, the President asked me if I would accept the position as the Director of the Secret Service. Not what I expected, not what I wanted, but it is a nice way to retire in two years. Besides, the Secret Service's relationship with the FBI could not be better since the new Director, Tom Wilson came aboard.

Our entire team—Jim, Tom, Steve, Judge Walters, General Monroe, Joe and I—spent a full afternoon with President Whitmore at his request. We spent a good portion of the time asking the President questions on the workings of the Sanchez White House. He was extremely candid and took the position that in hindsight, he should have asked more questions and been more involved in the decision-making. He stated that President Sanchez and Stewart Cohn spent countless hours alone in the Oval Office and believes that all of the planning and decisions came from those meetings. President Whitmore told us that he never was allowed into the inner circle by President Sanchez. Many times, he heard about appointments, to include the czar positions, after the decision was made.

Overall, it was a good meeting, with the President promising he would do everything in his power to ensure our Constitutional form of government is restored. He also stated that politics would never influence his decisions since he would be announcing that he will retire at the end of his term and not seek the election to a full term.

The country has not yet recovered from the aftermath of a corrupt administration and the shock of a presidential suicide. However, the new President has signed an Executive Order that requires full background investigations on all appointments to the White House, the Justice Department, and the Departments of Homeland Security and Defense. Congress has promised to make this a law during the upcoming session. I expect that for remainder of his term, this President will spend the majority of his time trying to re-establish the credibility of the federal government. If so, he certainly has his work cut out for him.

Washington will never be the same. Congress has initiated several investigations to ensure nothing like this can ever occur again. What is surprising is that they themselves have accepted part of the blame for what happened in the Sanchez Administration, for not insisting that all presidential appointees in sensitive positions be vetted. Each Senator and Representative has vowed that the Constitution will once again be the basis for our government and all it does. There also seems to be unprecedented cooperation between the political parties and for the time being, I expect that the protection and safety of America will be a top priority for Congress.

Although we have certainly tried and will continue to do so, we have not recovered the dirty bombs that President Sanchez and Cohn allowed into our country. I shudder to think that dirty bombs could actually be deployed against our citizens. Daily I ask that God may continue to bless and keep the United States of America safe.

"We have the power to make this the best generation of mankind in the history of the world or to make it the last."
—John F. Kennedy

EPILOGUE

TUESDAY, JANUARY 1

I ooked at the clock. It was 12:18 a.m. When my cell phone rings at this time in the early morning hours of the New Year, it is most likely not good news.

I was right—it wasn't.

"Let my name stand among those who are willing to bear ridicule and reproach for the truth's sake, and so earn some right to rejoice when the victory is won."
—Louisa May Alcott

MEET THE AUTHOR

CARL BAKER IS A VETERAN & SENIOR LAW ENFORCEMENT OFFICER

Carl Baker retired after 40 years in law enforcement and public safety. He served as a Colonel in both the New York State Police and the Virginia State Police, as Deputy Secretary of Public Safety to Virginia Governor George Allen, and as Chief of Police for Chesterfield County, VA. After retiring, he operated his own public safety consulting firm and was a Partner in Decide Smart, LLC. Carl is also a veteran of the U. S. Army, having served in both the Engineer Corps and Military Police Corps. A native of New York State, Carl and his wife, Katherine, now reside in The Villages, Florida.

YOUR NEXT GREAT
READ FROM
CARL R. BAKER
AND "THE DC SEVEN."

PATRIOTS'
CALL

A "DC Seven" Thriller

AVAILABLE
OCTOBER
2022.

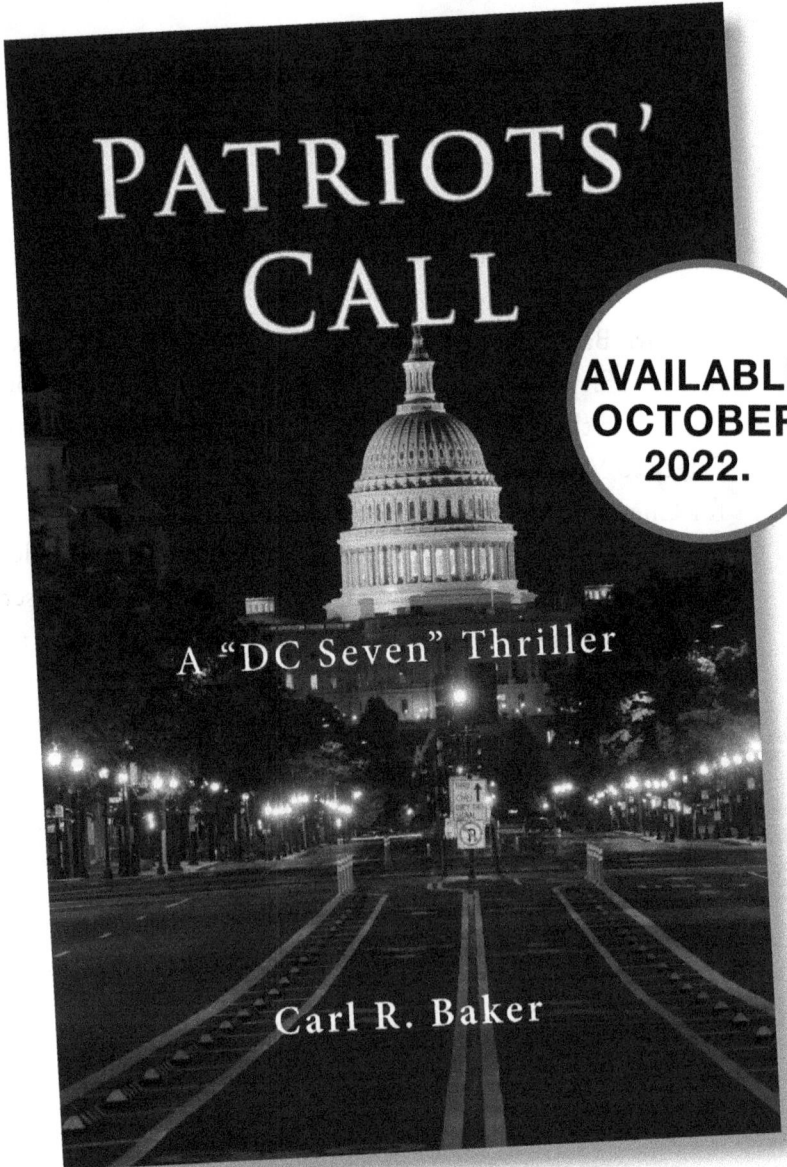

Carl R. Baker

It's 12 years later and a phone call brings "The DC Seven" back together to respond to an existential crisis.

The country is horribly divided, and the rifts are deepening. Someone is running the country, and it's not the newly elected President.

The real problem dividing the nation is "truth"— which version of "the truth" should people believe? With a highly partisan social media, biased news media, and fractured government agencies that seem to have become politicized, determining what is real has become almost impossible.

Violence, lack of leadership, and politicians more concerned with personal wealth than serving their constituents are the norm. The police have been rendered toothless, and inflation is running rampant.

Carl Baker brings "The DC Seven" story up-to-date in his latest book where the patriots follow up with solid police work and bring their own experience as events and threats attempt to bury the truth.

But averting collapse of the country will entail an enormous effort, sacrifice, and the unrelenting patriotism of the friends, their families, and the brave few who see the truth.

www.ingramcontent.com/pod-product-compliance
Lightning Source LLC
Chambersburg PA
CBHW070109030426
42335CB00016B/2069